AF701015

# CONCERT TOUR

## DESKTOP PUBLISHER

A Desktop Publishing Simulation

B.E. Publishing

ISBN 978-0-977461-16-5



Todd Toporski

Published by
B.E. Publishing
P.O. Box 8558
Warwick, RI 02888
U.S.A.

For more information,
visit www.bepublishing.com

**Copyright**

B.E. Publishing

**Concert Tour Desktop Publisher:**
*A Desktop Publishing Simulation*
Published by
B.E. Publishing

**Author**
Todd Toporski

**Editors**
Michael Gecawich
Kathleen Hicks

**Acknowledgements**
Marcy Toporski
Paul Owens
The Computer Students at Sparta High School



**ISBN: 978-0-977461-16-5**



**Permissions**
For permission to use materials from this text, please contact us by:

Tel: 888.781.6921
Fax: 401.781.7608
Email: permissions@bepublishing.com
Mail: B.E. Publishing
P.O. Box 8558 • Warwick, RI 02888 • U.S.A.

# Preface

Welcome to *Concert Tour Desktop Publisher*!

This simulation has been developed to provide desktop publishing and graphic design students with an in-depth, real-world experience in developing business documents using desktop publishing software. *Concert Tour Desktop Publisher* creates a scenario where the student takes on the role of the lead member and desktop publisher of his or her own band.

*Concert Tour Desktop Publisher* contains a collection of 16 projects that simulate the type of documents that are used to create a professional identity for real bands and music artists. This simulation also includes two additional "Encore" projects, which can be completed as extra credit projects. Use this book in conjunction with your instructor's guidance and your desktop publishing software. The material represented in *Concert Tour Desktop Publisher* is generic and can be completed using any desktop publishing software, such as Adobe InDesign, Microsoft Publisher, or Google Drawings.

This simulation will challenge your desktop publishing and graphic design skills as you create your band's professional identity, plan concerts, publicize the band, sign a recording contract, and plan a concert tour.

*Concert Tour Desktop Publisher* will challenge your design and page layout skills by presenting a wide variety of documents to complete. From designing a concert T-shirt, to creating a fan club newsletter, you will gain real-world experience in using the following skills:

- Page layout and design
- Creativity and imagination
- Critical thinking
- Establishing a business identity
- Advertising and marketing
- Planning and decision-making
- Completing a comprehensive project
- Searching and using content from the Internet

So, get ready to hit the stage! Soon you will be getting your desktop publishing skills rockin' and rollin' in the *Concert Tour Desktop Publisher* simulation.

## About the Author

Todd Toporski is a high school computer teacher at Sparta High School in Sparta, Michigan. In Mr. Toporski's seventeen-year teaching tenure, he has taught a variety of computer courses including Microsoft Office Applications, Web Site Design, Desktop Publishing, and Computer Programming.

An advocate for technology, Toporski has presented numerous technology-related workshops at the Michigan Association for Computer Users in Learning conference, the Michigan Governor's Conference on Quality in Education, and the Michigan Alternative Education Organization conference.

Toporski has been recognized for his creativity and "learn-by-doing" philosophy in the classroom. He is a two-time recipient of the TAPS Award (Technology for Authentic Problem Solving) and was recently presented with the Ameritech STAR award (School Technology Achievement Recognition).

He holds a Bachelor of Science degree in Business Education and a Master of Arts degree in Educational Leadership.

# Table of Contents



CONCERT TOUR DESKTOP PUBLISHER

# Table of Contents (continued)

# SECTION ONE: INTRODUCTION

CONCERT TOUR
DESKTOP PUBLISHER

INCLUDED IN THIS SECTION:

## 1.1 Welcome to Concert Tour Desktop Publisher

Just about everyone has dreamt of being in his or her own music band. In *Concert Tour Desktop Publisher*, now you can fulfill your dream. *Concert Tour Desktop Publisher* is a fun and exciting desktop publishing simulation designed to let you (the student) take the music stage as the star of your own band.

*Concert Tour Desktop Publisher* will give you an in-depth, real-world view of what it's like to use desktop publishing software to create and design documents to market and promote a real product (your own band). After creating your own band name and logo, your quest will be to create and design a variety of promotional documents that will propel your band to national-star status. From concert Frisbees and tickets, to a fan club newsletter and CD covers, you will be challenged to use your desktop publishing, technical writing, creativity, and design skills to create a professional identity for your band.

With that said, it's time to get ready to take the stage. So put on your creative thinking cap and sharpen your design pencils—it's time for *Concert Tour Desktop Publisher*.

## 1.2 Your Role as a Concert Tour Desktop Publisher

*The scenario you will follow for Concert Tour Desktop Publisher is as follows:*

> *You've started your own music band. Your band has spent the last two years out in your parents' garage playing, practicing, and writing songs. Unfortunately, no one has noticed. That's where the Concert Tour Desktop Publishing simulation comes in.*
>
> *In this simulation, you will get your band "out of the garage" and into the public eye. To achieve success for your band, you'll be asked to create a series of promotional documents to give your band a professional image and get it noticed. By using your creativity and desktop publishing design skills, you'll be taking the stage, performing a free concert to gain publicity, receiving a recording contract, and eventually taking your act on a national concert tour.*
>
> *By completing the projects in this simulation, you will fine-tune your desktop publishing, creativity, and design skills and learn what it's like to market and promote a real product—your own music band!*

## 1.3 The Skills You Will Be Drawing On Throughout This Simulation

The following is a list of the major skills you will be drawing on throughout this simulation:

- Creating a band name and logo
- Page layout and design
- Working with graphic images, objects, text, and elements used in graphic design
- Creativity and imagination
- Technical writing
- Critical thinking
- Establishing a real-world product identity and image
- Advertising and marketing
- Planning and decision-making
- The ability to complete a comprehensive real-world, long-term project

## 1.4 What You'll Be Asked to Design

*Concert Tour Desktop Publisher* is divided into six parts and includes a series of 16 projects and 2 extra credit projects. The table below provides a list of each part along with the corresponding projects that you will be required to create and design throughout this simulation.

**Note:** *Based on your teacher's instructions, you may be asked to complete all or only a portion of the projects listed below.*

**A List of the Projects You Will Be Completing in Concert Tour Desktop Publisher:**

**Part 1: The Audition**
- Project 1: Creating Your Band and Getting It Approved

**Part 2: The Opening Act**
- Project 2: Design a Logo for Your Band
- Project 3: Design a Business Card for Your Band
- Project 4: Design Letterhead for Your Band
- Project 5: Design an Envelope for Your Band

**Part 3: The Free Concert**
- Project 6: Design a Concert Flyer
- Project 7: Design a Concert T-shirt
- Project 8: Design a Bumper Sticker for Your Band
- Project 9: Design a Promotional Concert Frisbee

**Part 4: Your Band Gets Discovered**
- Project 10: Design a CD Jewel Case
- Project 11: Design a Poster for Your Band
- Project 12: Design a Fan Club Newsletter
- Project 13: Design a Fan Club Member Card

**Part 5: Your Band Goes on Tour**
- Project 14: Design a Three-Panel Brochure
- Project 15: Design a Concert Ticket
- Project 16: Design a Billboard Advertisement

**Part 6: The Encore (Extra Credit)**
- Project 17: Design a Backstage Pass
- Project 18: Create a Tour Bus Design

## 1.5 Prerequisite Skills

In order to complete this simulation, the student must possess a basic working knowledge of the following:

- A desktop publishing software
- An illustration or drawing software
- Familiarity with working with files

**Note:** *The instructions included within each project in this simulation have been generalized and are not specific to any one particular desktop publishing software application.*

## 1.6 Materials Required to Complete This Simulation

In order to complete the projects in this simulation, you will need the following:

- A computer and printer
- Any desktop publishing software application
- Any illustration or drawing software application
- Any word processing software application
- Copies of the *Concert Tour Document Planning Form* and the *Band Planning Form*

## 1.7 Important Notes For The Instructor

*Concert Tour Desktop Publisher* is designed as a self-guided, long-term independent project. The instructor's main role during this simulation is one of a facilitator. In this simulation, it is assumed that students already possess most or all of the desktop publishing skills required to complete each project. This simulation is intended to be used as a final assessment tool of students' knowledge and understanding of desktop publishing software.

To provide students with a visual design guide for each project, this simulation includes a series of documents produced by a sample band titled "Stonehenge." The sample documents have been included to provide students with layout and design ideas. They are intended to be used for "design inspiration" purposes only. The student should not copy the design and content of the sample documents provided. The final design and content of each document produced should be creative and unique to each student, allowing them to showcase their own creativity and design skills.

**In *Concert Tour Desktop Publisher*, the instructor's primary tasks are to:**

- Introduce the simulation to students.
- Approve each student's selected band and logo. (See Project 1 in the simulation for more details.)
- Provide students with technical assistance when needed.
- Keep students on task throughout the simulation.
- Introduce each project in the simulation.
- Ensure that students do not copy the design and content from the sample documents provided by the sample band "Stonehenge."
- Assess student work.

See the *Concert Tour Desktop Publisher Teacher's Guide* for more information about assisting and assessing students in this simulation.

# SECTION TWO: USING THIS BOOK AND YOUR DESKTOP PUBLISHING SOFTWARE

CONCERT TOUR
DESKTOP PUBLISHER

## INCLUDED IN THIS SECTION:

## 2.1 Understanding the Format of This Book

This simulation has been organized into an easy-to-read, self-guided, step-by-step format that includes a total of 16 projects and 2 extra credit projects. What follows is a brief explanation of the individual sections that make up each part of the simulation. Read this section thoroughly to help become familiar with the format of this book.

## 2.2 How Each Project is Organized

### Simulation Part Dividers:

This simulation is divided into six parts. Each part includes a title page that lists the projects included within it.

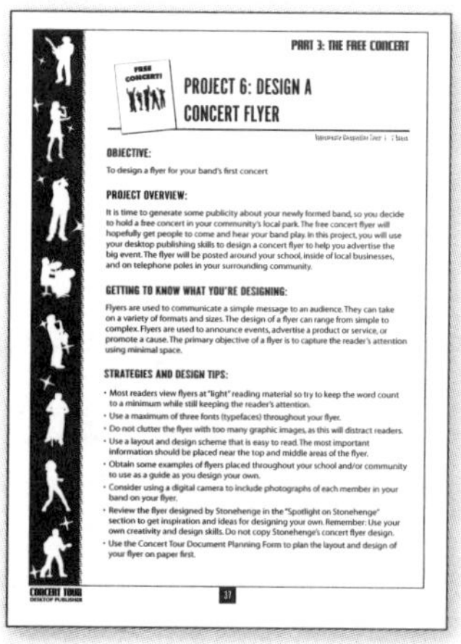


### Project Title Page:

Each new project begins with a project title page. The project title page includes the following headings:

- **Project Title:**
  Provides the title of each project.
- **Approximate Completion Time:**
  The approximate amount of time (in hours) it will take to complete each project.
- **Objective:**
  The objective of each project.
- **Project Overview:**
  A description of the document to be created along with the purpose of how the document will be used.
- **Getting to Know What You're Designing:**
  A detailed description of the document to be created.
- **Strategies and Design Tips:**
  Strategies and design tips to assist in the creation of each document.

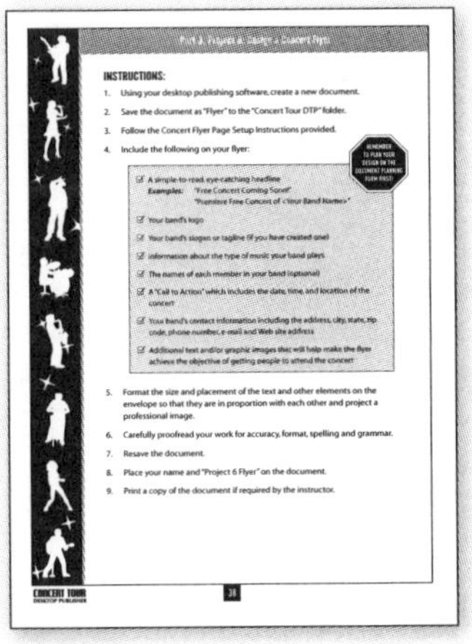


## Project Instructions:

Provides step-by-step instructions to follow to complete each project.

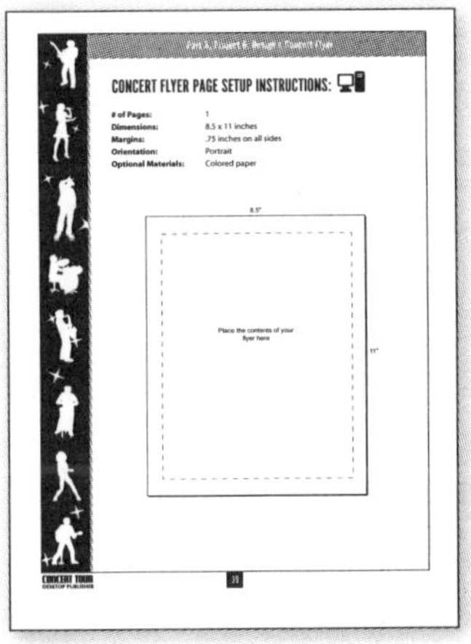


## Project Page Setup Instructions:

Provides information and instructions about how to set up each new project document using your desktop publishing software.

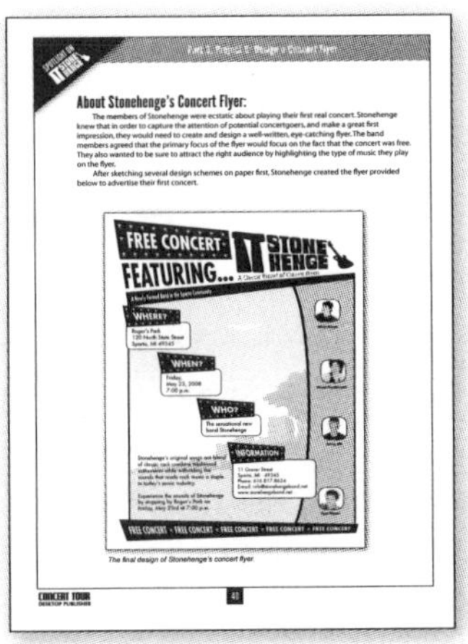


## Spotlight on Stonehenge:

Provides sample documents at the end of each project using the sample band "Stonehenge." More information about the sample band is provided in *Section 3: Meet Stonehenge.*

## 2.3 Using the Band Planning Form

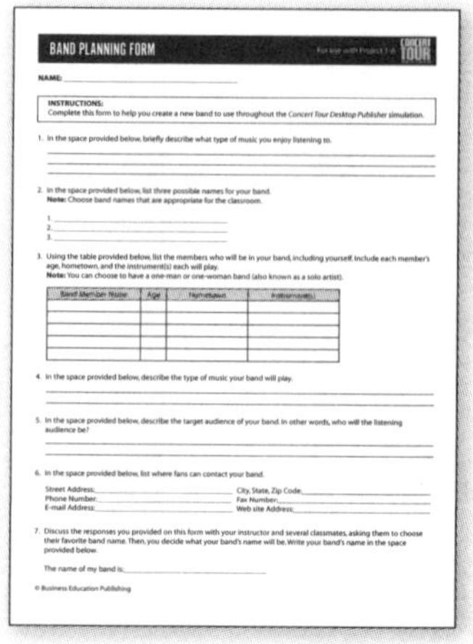


In Project 1, you will be asked to complete a *Band Planning Form* to assist you in selecting your new band, which will be used throughout the simulation. You will be required to submit the *Band Planning Form* (shown on **page 11**) to your instructor to obtain approval before continuing on with the simulation. You can obtain a copy of the *Band Planning Form* from your instructor.

## 2.4 Using the Concert Tour Document Planning Form

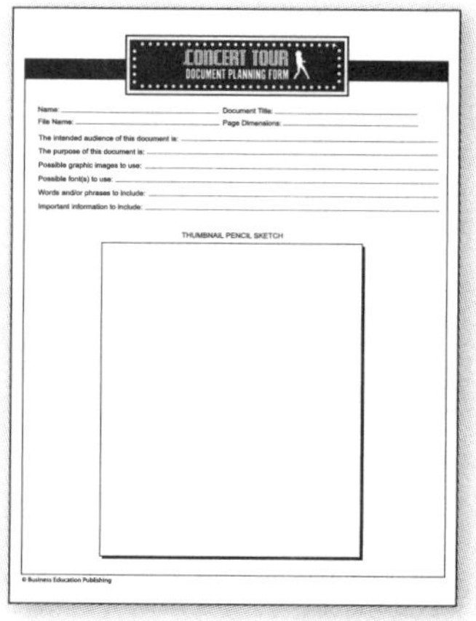


Good designers always plan on paper first. To assist you in planning the layout and design of each document you will create, a *Concert Tour Document Planning Form* is provided on **page 12**. It is recommended that you use the *Concert Tour Document Planning Form* to plan each document on paper before starting its design on the computer. You can obtain copies of this form from your instructor.

## 2.5 Saving Your Project Files

It is important that the project files in this simulation are saved in the same folder on your hard drive or network drive. Follow the instructions provided below to be sure your computer is set up properly before beginning this simulation.

IMPORTANT !

**Before beginning this simulation, do the following:**

Create a new folder on your hard drive or network drive titled *"Concert Tour DTP."* All completed project files should be saved to this folder using the file names provided in the instructions within each project.

# BAND PLANNING FORM

For use with Project 1-A

**NAME:** ______________________________

**INSTRUCTIONS:**
Complete this form to help you create a new band to use throughout the *Concert Tour Desktop Publisher* simulation.

1. In the space provided below, briefly describe what type of music you enjoy listening to.

______________________________
______________________________
______________________________

2. In the space provided below, list three possible names for your band.
**Note:** Choose band names that are appropriate for the classroom.

1. ______________________________
2. ______________________________
3. ______________________________

3. Using the table provided below, list the members who will be in your band, including yourself. Include each member's age, hometown, and the instrument(s) each will play.
**Note:** You can choose to have a one-man or one-woman band (also known as a solo artist).

| Band Member Name | Age | Hometown | Instrument(s) |
|---|---|---|---|
| | | | |
| | | | |
| | | | |
| | | | |
| | | | |

4. In the space provided below, describe the type of music your band will play.

______________________________
______________________________

5. In the space provided below, describe the target audience of your band. In other words, who will the listening audience be?

______________________________
______________________________

6. In the space provided below, list where fans can contact your band.

Street Address: ______________________________
City, State, Zip Code: ______________________________
Phone Number: ______________________________
Fax Number: ______________________________
E-mail Address: ______________________________
Web site Address: ______________________________

7. Discuss the responses you provided on this form with your instructor and several classmates, asking them to choose their favorite band name. Then, you decide what your band's name will be. Write your band's name in the space provided below.

The name of my band is: ______________________________

# CONCERT TOUR
## DOCUMENT PLANNING FORM

Name: ______________________ Document Title: ______________________

File Name: ______________________ Page Dimensions: ______________________

The intended audience of this document is: ______________________

The purpose of this document is: ______________________

Possible graphic images to use: ______________________

Possible font(s) to use: ______________________

Words and/or phrases to include: ______________________

Important information to include: ______________________

THUMBNAIL PENCIL SKETCH

# SECTION THREE: MEET STONEHENGE

## YOUR CONCERT TOUR GUIDE BAND

CONCERT TOUR
DESKTOP PUBLISHER

### INCLUDED IN THIS SECTION:

## 3.1 Who is Stonehenge?

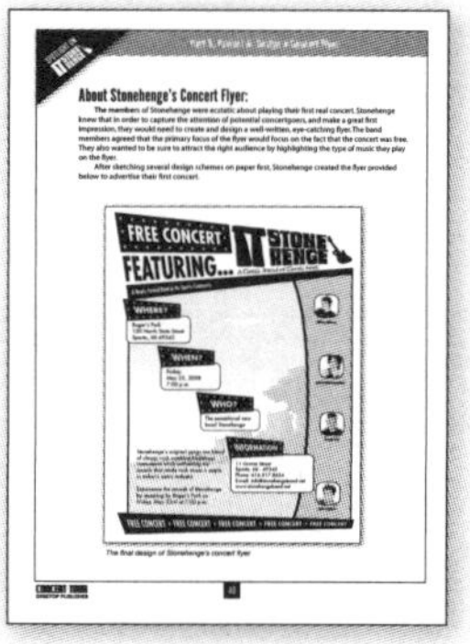
About Stonehenge's Concert Flyer:

FREE CONCERT FEATURING...

Stonehenge is a band that was created specifically for this simulation. Stonehenge will serve as your concert tour guide throughout this simulation by providing you with sample documents for each project in the simulation.

As you work through this simulation, you will be able to follow Stonehenge's progress right along with your own. At the conclusion of each individual project in the simulation, you will see a "Spotlight on Stonehenge" section. Here, you can learn how Stonehenge arrived at the design of the sample document provided. The sample Stonehenge documents are included to provide you with design ideas, content, and inspiration for creating your own document.

IMPORTANT !

**DO NOT COPY THE SAMPLE STONEHENGE DOCUMENTS!**

The sample documents provided by the band Stonehenge are intended to serve only as a guide to the student. The layout and design schemes provided in the Stonehenge documents should not be copied or duplicated. Remember, to create your own band's identity, you should utilize your own creativity, imagination, and design talents. Copycat bands never make it!

## 3.2 How Stonehenge Was Formed

Several high school classmates attending Sparta High School in Sparta, Michigan, formed the band Stonehenge in November 2007. During her sophomore year, Alexis Montgomery, the band's current lead singer and side-guitarist, decided that she wanted to take her singing talent to the stage. Alexis posted flyers throughout her school petitioning musically talented students to try out to be in her band. After surveying more than 30 prospective band members, Stonehenge was formed when Alexis acquired three classmates to enlist in the band.

The name Stonehenge was the brainchild of Mitch Mason, the band's lead guitarist, who was intrigued by the name while enrolled in a World History course. Stonehenge is a mysterious ancient monument of huge stones standing on the Salisbury Plain in Wiltshire, England. Its purpose and structure has captured imaginations for centuries.

Because the band's focus will be on playing smooth, classic rock music, the name Stonehenge was a perfect fit.

## 3.3 Meet the Members of Stonehenge

**Alexis Montgomery**

Alexis is the lead singer of the band. She co-writes most of the music with Mitch. She is a 17-year-old high school junior who aspires to pursue music in college and is the founder of Stonehenge. Alexis is also very talented in graphic design and will be designing the band's logo and other identity documents that will hopefully help to get the band noticed by a recording company.

**Mitch Mason**

Also a junior in high school, Mitch is the band's lead guitarist. He taught himself to play guitar in elementary school and has been playing ever since. He co-writes the band's music with Alexis. He currently works part-time as a guitar instructor at a local music store. Mitch's best friend is Corey Hill, the band's drummer. Mitch hopes that Stonehenge will get noticed so that he can continue playing with them after graduating from high school. As a fall back, Mitch plans to major in business management in college.

**Kyle Wilson**

Kyle is the bass player for Stonehenge and sings backup vocals. He met Alexis in a class they had together his freshman year. He is a 16-year-old sophomore, and is currently the bass player in his school's jazz band. He hopes that his role in Stonehenge will be long-lasting, and is happy to be playing music in an organized band.

**Corey Hill**

Corey plays the drums and bongos for the band and also sings backup vocals. He is a 17-year-old junior who started playing the drums in his freshman year. Corey is a straight "A" student who has the self-discipline to maintain a part-time job, practice with the band, and play a variety of sports at his school.

## 3.4 The Future of Stonehenge

Alexis Montgomery and her band are trying to hit it big and go on a national concert tour. They practice in her parents' garage, write songs, and are waiting for their big break. Alexis has decided that in order to move the band to the next level, the band needs to create a professional image and identity.

Since the band has generated almost no income and cannot afford to hire a professional graphic designer, Alexis has decided to take on the role of desktop publisher for her band. She will create and design the necessary documents that can help Stonehenge land a recording contract and hopefully go on a national concert tour.

Throughout this simulation, you will be provided with the actual documents that Alexis has created to give Stonehenge their professional image and identity. Just like you, the members of Stonehenge are hoping to get noticed, build a fan base, and get their music and name "out there" for the public to see and hear.

# SECTION FOUR: DTP TIPS AND GUIDELINES FOR MAKING YOUR BAND FAMOUS

CONCERT TOUR
DESKTOP PUBLISHER

**INCLUDED IN THIS SECTION:**

## 4.1 The Importance of Knowing Good Design Techniques

Whether you're an experienced graphic designer or you're just getting started, reading the desktop publishing design tips and guidelines provided in this section will help you in the preparation of each document in the *Concert Tour Desktop Publisher* simulation. Careful preparation, planning, and following these guidelines will help you create professional, attractive, eye-catching documents that will showcase your new band in this simulation.

## 4.2 Elements of a Well-Designed Document

The following is a checklist of items that will make a document sparkle and shine with professionalism and creativity:

- The document is attractive and pleasing to look at and read.
- The document is well-organized.
- The document is self-explanatory.
- The text and imagery are carefully linked to each other.
- The design and content are appropriate for the targeted audience.

What follows are some fundamental desktop publishing design tips, guidelines, and advice to follow as you produce each document throughout this simulation. Following these tips and guidelines will help you to produce a series of promotional documents that will propel your band to national stardom!

# 4.3 Desktop Publishing Tips and Guidelines To Help Make Your Band Famous

## Desktop Publishing Tips and Guidelines

### TIP #1: KNOW YOUR AUDIENCE

Determine the single most important message of your document by asking yourself: If my viewer carries away one idea, what do I want it to be? The answer will be the central theme that determines your entire document design.

### TIP #2: USE THE RIGHT AMOUNT OF WHITE SPACE

White space is the area of a document not covered by text or graphics. The general rule of thumb when considering white space is not to have too much or the viewer's eye will wander, and not to have too little or you'll confuse and overwhelm your viewer. A guideline to follow is that if your page looks cluttered, eliminate the least important text and/or graphic images from the page.

### TIP #3: USE MINIMAL TYPEFACES (FONTS)

Take a look at your favorite magazine or book. Chances are they contain no more than two to three typefaces (more commonly referred to as fonts) in total. Too many typefaces or fonts will make your document look cluttered, unprofessional, and difficult to read.

As a rule, stick to using no more than a total of two to three fonts per document. Select one font that will serve as the primary font (used for areas that contain more than two or three sentences in one area) and one font to serve as your secondary font (used for areas that are headlines, headings, or subheadings).

**Here are some general guidelines to follow when working with typefaces (fonts) and type styles:**

*Rule 1:* Font size should be kept between 18-24 points for headlines, 14-16 points for subheadings, and between 10-12 points for text used in the body areas of a document.
*Rule 2:* When considering type styles, with the exception of titles, avoid using all capital letters.
*Rule 3:* Avoid excessive use of underlined, italicized, and boldfaced text.
*Rule 4:* Select a typeface (font) that is appropriate to the document's subject.
*Rule 5:* Be consistent with your typeface (font) choices throughout each document in the simulation. This will help to establish a consistent look, adding to the professionalism of the document.

### TIP #4: KEEP EVERYTHING IN PROPORTION

Creating balance and symmetry throughout a document is critical to its final appearance. If, for example, you are creating a document that contains three separate headings, keep the type size of the headings relatively the same. Otherwise, your document will look out of proportion, giving it an amateur look and feel.

**Follow these guidelines to keep your documents looking balanced and in proportion:**

- Use the same typefaces (fonts) throughout each document to give the document a crisp, clean, consistent look.
- If using columns, keep the width and the distance between each column the same.
- Use the same style and size graphic images.
- Use the same type size for different headings and the same type size for body areas.

## Desktop Publishing Tips and Guidelines (continued)

### TIP #5: USE PAGE MARGINS AND SPACING WISELY

All edges and margins of a document should be straight and even. Don't overcrowd space, and be attentive to balance content from top to bottom and side-margin to side-margin. If possible, organize your text into columns, rather than stretching it across the page. This will make the text easier to read and give the document a more balanced appearance.

### TIP #6: CHOOSE THE RIGHT GRAPHICS

You've heard it a million times, "a picture is worth a thousand words." How true this is when it comes to document design. When selecting graphic images, try choosing those that have the same look and style. For instance, let's say you're designing the band brochure and you've selected a graphic image of a guitar that has a photographic style. Other graphics that you choose to use in the brochure should have the same photographic quality in them. This helps to establish consistency throughout the document and gives it a polished, professional look.

### TIP #7: ESTABLISH A PROFESSIONAL IDENTITY

When businesses communicate through print, they rely heavily on the look and design of their documents to convey their intended image and identity to consumers.

**To help your band establish a professional image throughout the simulation, you should:**

- Use the same typefaces (fonts) throughout the simulation.
- Use the same color scheme (if using a color printer).
- Use the same style of objects and design elements.
- Use the same style graphic images.

### TIP #8: PROOFREAD FOR SPELLING, GRAMMAR, AND DESIGN

Nothing spoils a well-designed document more than a typo. When you are nearing the completion of a document, take the time to proofread it for spelling, grammar, and design. Are there any misspelled words? Do the sentences make sense? Did you leave out any required text or design elements? These are the questions to ask before submitting any document.

A good piece of advice is to give your document to one or two people and let them proofread the document. Often they will find an error or omission that you didn't see.

### TIP #9: REVISE, REVISE, REVISE

Desktop publishing design is much like writing an essay. It almost never comes out right the first time around. Look at your starting point as just that, a starting point. Print your document early on in the design phase and plan on making several revisions, additions, and deletions to attain a professional, well-designed end product.

### TIP #10: HAVE A PAPER PLAN

One of the worst habits a desktop publisher or designer can establish is to start designing on a computer without first having a plan on paper. Good design starts on paper first! A sheet of paper, a pencil, and a ruler are the only tools you'll need to get your imagination and creativity steamrolling. Look at it this way—it is much easier, and faster, to experiment with shapes, graphics, text styles, and borders on a piece of paper than on a computer.

Using the *Concert Tour Document Planning Form* will help you to create a good paper plan of your band's documents before creating them on the computer.

# SECTION FIVE: TIME TO TAKE THE STAGE

Now that you have familiarized yourself with the Concert Tour Desktop Publisher simulation, it's time to take to the stage and begin the journey of taking your band on a national concert tour. The remainder of this book is divided into six parts, which are listed below. Each part contains the individual projects that you will complete throughout the simulation.

Good luck as you take on the role of your band's own concert tour desktop publisher!

CONCERT TOUR
DESKTOP PUBLISHER

## THE INDIVIDUAL PARTS OF THE SIMULATION:

### PART 1: THE AUDITION
Project 1: Creating Your Band and Getting It Approved

### PART 2: THE OPENING ACT
Project 2: Design a Logo for Your Band
Project 3: Design a Business Card for Your Band
Project 4: Design Letterhead for Your Band
Project 5: Design an Envelope for Your Band

### PART 3: THE FREE CONCERT
Project 6: Design a Concert Flyer
Project 7: Design a Concert T-shirt
Project 8: Design a Bumper Sticker for Your Band
Project 9: Design a Promotional Concert Frisbee

### PART 4: YOUR BAND GETS DISCOVERED
Project 10: Design a CD Jewel Case
Project 11: Design a Poster for Your Band
Project 12: Design a Fan Club Newsletter
Project 13: Design a Fan Club Member Card

### PART 5: YOUR BAND GOES ON TOUR
Project 14: Design a Three-Panel Brochure
Project 15: Design a Concert Ticket
Project 16: Design a Billboard Advertisement

### PART 6: THE ENCORE (EXTRA CREDIT)
Project 17: Design a Backstage Pass
Project 18: Create a Tour Bus Design

# PART 1: THE AUDITION

CONCERT TOUR
DESKTOP PUBLISHER

## PROJECTS INCLUDED:

**Project 1: Creating Your Band and Getting it Approved**

- 1-A: Creating Your Band Using the "Band Planning Form"
- 1-B: Creating a Memo to Your Instructor to Obtain Approval to Use Your Band

# PROJECT 1: CREATING YOUR BAND AND GETTING IT APPROVED

Approximate Completion Time: 1 hour

## OBJECTIVE:

- To create your concert tour band
- To obtain approval of your band from your instructor

## PROJECT OVERVIEW:

Before you can take to the stage and participate in this simulation, you must create your own fictitious concert band and obtain permission to use it by your instructor. This project is divided into the following two parts:

**Project 1-A: Creating Your Band Using the "Band Planning Form"**
**Project 1-B: Creating a Memo to Your Instructor to Obtain Approval to Use Your Band**

## Project 1-A: Creating Your Band Using the "Band Planning Form"

## INSTRUCTIONS:

1. Obtain a copy of the *Band Planning Form* from your instructor.

   **Note:** *You can choose to create a one-man or one-woman band or a band with more than one member.*

2. Carefully complete the *Band Planning Form*.

   **Note:** *The details you provide on the Band Planning Form will be used throughout the remainder of this simulation. Take your time in completing this form.*

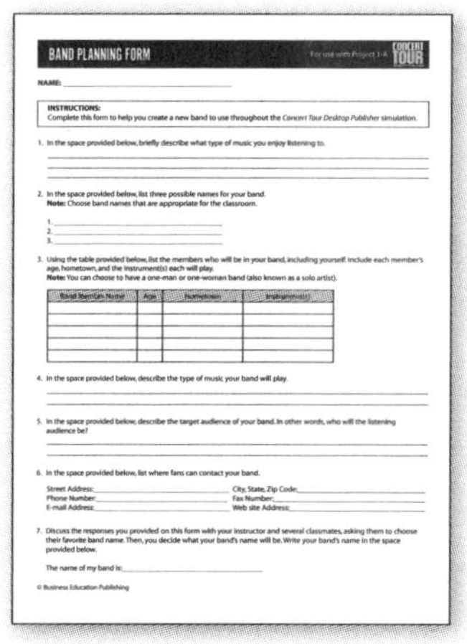

## Project 1-B: Creating a Memo to Your Instructor to Obtain Approval to Use Your Band

### INSTRUCTIONS:

1. Using a word processing software application such as Microsoft Word, create a new document.
2. Save the document as "Instructor Memo" to the "Concert Tour DTP" folder.
3. Type and format a memo to your instructor following the template provided in **Figure 1.1**.
4. Carefully proofread your work for accuracy, format, spelling, and grammar.
5. Resave the document.
6. Print a copy of the document for your instructor.

**Figure 1.1**

# MEMO

To: [Your Instructor's Name]

From: [Your Name]

Date: [Current Date]

Subject: Concert Tour Desktop Publisher Band Approval

As you are aware, I am in the process of completing the *Concert Tour Desktop Publisher* simulation. In order to continue with the simulation, I am required to create my own band. Please review the proposed band provided below. Please indicate if I have your approval to use the proposed band by completing the bottom portion of this memo and returning it to me.

**Proposed Band:**
The name of my proposed band is [***band name***]. The type of music my band will play is [***type of music***].

The members of my band and the instruments/role each will play are [***list all band member names and instruments/role each will play***].

---

____ I approve this band for use in the *Concert Tour Desktop Publisher* simulation.

____ I do not approve this band for use in the *Concert Tour Desktop Publisher* simulation.

____ Instructor Initials

*Instructor: Please return this form to the student after approving or not approving the proposed band.*

# PART 2: THE OPENING ACT

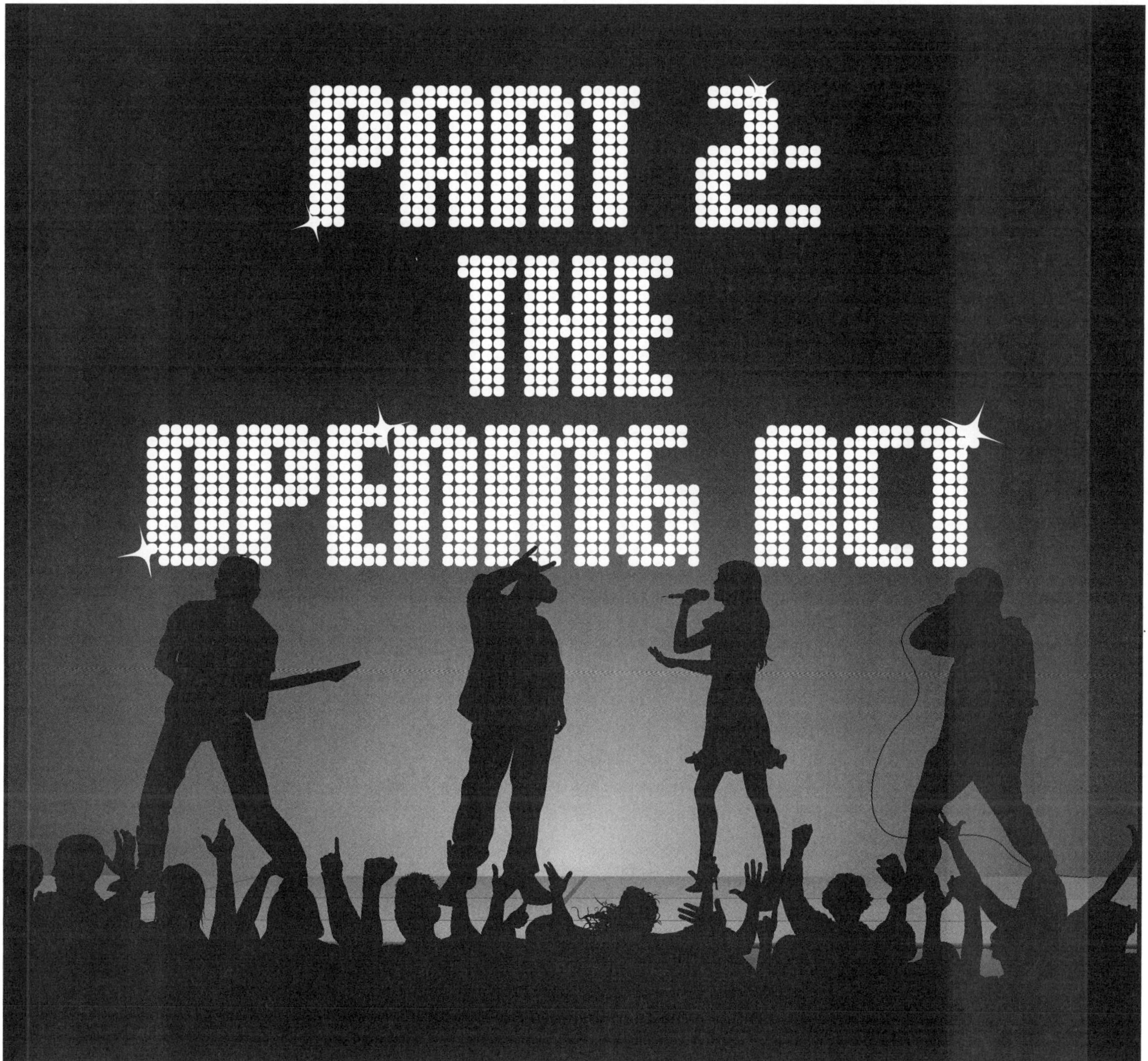

CONCERT TOUR
DESKTOP PUBLISHER

## PROJECTS INCLUDED:

Project 2: Design a Logo for Your Band
Project 3: Design a Business Card for Your Band
Project 4: Design Letterhead for Your Band
Project 5: Design an Envelope for Your Band

# PROJECT 2: DESIGN A LOGO FOR YOUR BAND

Approximate Completion Time: 1 - 2 hours

## OBJECTIVE:

To create and design a logo for your band

## PROJECT OVERVIEW:

All businesses should have a recognizable logo that customers identify with; your band is no different. You need to develop a band logo that you can use with different documents throughout this simulation and that fans will recognize and immediately connect to your band.

## GETTING TO KNOW WHAT YOU'RE DESIGNING:

A logo is a name, symbol, emblem, or trademark designed for easy and definite recognition. In short, a logo is one of the most important elements in defining an image for a company. A logo can contain text, graphics, or a combination of both.

## STRATEGIES AND DESIGN TIPS:

- Take your time in designing your logo, as it is the most important element in creating your band's identity and image. The logo will be used in all future projects.
- Search the Internet for famous bands and analyze the design of their logos. Take note of the fonts (typefaces) and colors each band uses.
- Identify one or two appropriate fonts (typefaces) to use in your logo.
- Experiment with one or two colors to incorporate in your logo if you will be printing using a color printer.
- Experiment with grey scale colors if you will be printing using a monochrome (black ink only) printer.
- Browse a variety of possible clipart images to use in your logo that will help fans to identify with the band.
- Review the logo designed by Stonehenge in the "Spotlight on Stonehenge" section to get inspiration and design ideas for your logo. *Remember:* Use your own creativity and design skills. Do not copy Stonehenge's logo.
- Use a blank sheet of paper to sketch several possible logo designs for your band before creating one on the computer.

## INSTRUCTIONS:

1. Using a blank sheet of paper and a pencil, sketch five different logo designs for your band.
2. Using the paper-sketched logos you created in Step 1, survey your instructor and several classmates asking them to select their favorite logo.
3. Select a final logo to use for your band.
4. Using an illustration or drawing software program such as Adobe Illustrator, Adobe Photoshop, Microsoft Paint, or any graphics software, create a new document.
5. Using the sketched logo you selected, create your band's logo.

   **Note:** *Be sure to design your logo large enough in size so that it can be resized and scaled without losing quality and resolution.*
6. Carefully proofread your work for accuracy, format, spelling, and grammar.
7. Save the logo as "Band Logo" to the "Concert Tour DTP" folder.

   **Note:** *You will be required to use your logo in many of the projects you will be designing in this simulation. Save the logo in a format that will allow you to import/insert it as a graphic image in your desktop publishing software. Common formats are JPEG, TIFF, or BMP. Consult with your instructor if you are unsure of which format to use.*
8. Print a copy of the document if required by the instructor.

## About Stonehenge's Logos:

Below are the five logo designs that Stonehenge considered using for their band. Notice how the band worked with using the famous Stonehenge rock symbol and a guitar to incorporate into the text part of their logo.

*Possible logo designs created by Stonehenge.*

After surveying their family, friends, classmates, and fans, Stonehenge decided to use the logo shown below for their band.

*The final logo design chosen by Stonehenge.*

BUSINESS CARD

# PROJECT 3: DESIGN A BUSINESS CARD FOR YOUR BAND

Approximate Completion Time: .5 hours

## OBJECTIVE:

To create and design a business card for your band

## PROJECT OVERVIEW:

As you begin the task of publicizing your band and looking for places to play, you will be talking to club owners, agents, recording-industry executives, radio personalities, and prospective fans. You will need something to give these people so that they remember you, your band, and your contact information. In this project, you will use your desktop publishing skills to design a professional business card that will help project your band's identity and image.

## GETTING TO KNOW WHAT YOU'RE DESIGNING:

A business card is a small printed card usually containing a person's name, business affiliation, job title, address, telephone number, fax number, and e-mail/Web site address. The purpose of a business card is to announce one's identity, presence, and the intention to conduct business. The business card is perhaps the most widely used mini-document in the business world. A business card is the handshake you leave behind after meeting someone in the professional world.

## STRATEGIES AND DESIGN TIPS:

- Business cards present a lot of information in a small space. Utilize the space on your business card to highlight the most important information, such as the band logo, your name, and contact information.
- Avoid cluttering your business card and allow for plenty of white space to maximize readability.
- Obtain examples of real business cards to use as a guide in designing your own.
- The overall look and feel of your business card should match the style and design of your band's logo.
- Use a maximum of one or two fonts (typefaces) on your business card.
- Review the business card designed by Stonehenge in the "Spotlight on Stonehenge" section to get inspiration and ideas for designing your own. *Remember:* Use your own creativity and design skills. Do not copy Stonehenge's business card design.
- Use the "Concert Tour Document Planning Form" to plan the layout and design of your business card on paper first.

## INSTRUCTIONS:

1. Using your desktop publishing software, create a new document.
2. Save the document as "Business Card" to the "Concert Tour DTP" folder.
3. Follow the Business Card Page Setup Instructions provided on the next page.
4. Include the following on your business card:

REMEMBER TO PLAN YOUR DESIGN ON THE DOCUMENT PLANNING FORM FIRST!

- ☑ Your band's logo
- ☑ Your band's slogan or tagline (if you have created one)
- ☑ Your name and title
- ☑ The names of the additional members in your band (optional, if room permits)
- ☑ Contact information including your band's address, city, state, zip code, phone number, fax number, e-mail address, and Web site address
- ☑ Additional graphic images and/or a border (optional, if room permits)

5. Format the size and placement of the text and other elements on the business card so that they are in proportion with each other and project a professional image.
6. Carefully proofread your work for accuracy, format, spelling, and grammar.
7. Resave the document.
8. Print a copy of the document.
9. Write your name and "Project 3 Business Card" on the document.

# BUSINESS CARD PAGE SETUP INSTRUCTIONS:

| | |
|---|---|
| **# of Pages:** | 1 |
| **Dimensions:** | 8.5 x 11 inches |
| **Margins:** | 1 inch on all sides |
| **Orientation:** | Portrait |
| **Optional Materials:** | Cardstock paper |
| **Other:** | Using the rectangle tool in your desktop publishing software, draw a rectangle that measures 3.5 inches wide by 2 inches high. Place the rectangle in the center of the page. The rectangle represents the business card on your page. Place the contents of the business card within this rectangle. |

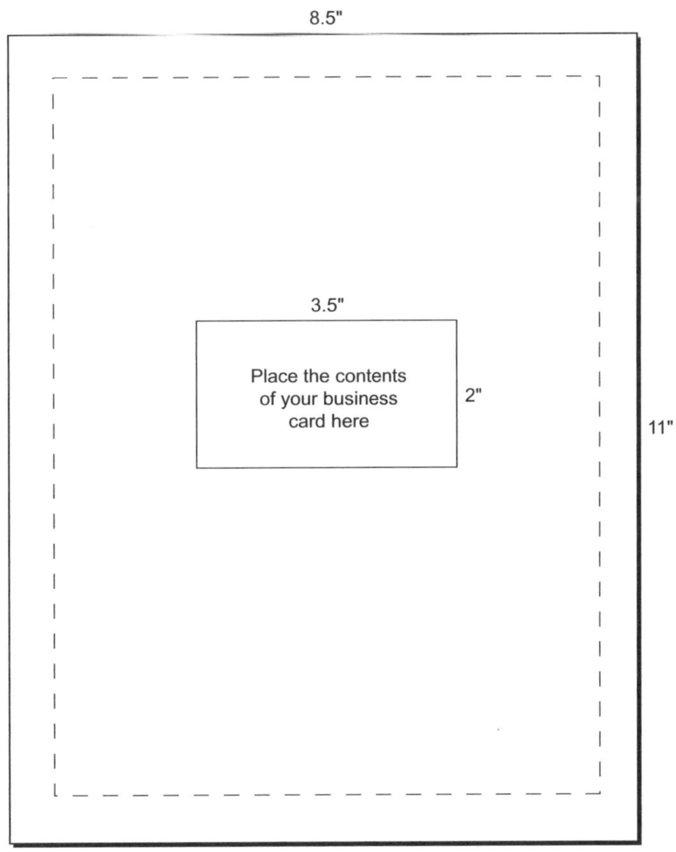

# About Stonehenge's Business Card:

With the band logo complete, the business card design for Stonehenge was easy. Provided below is the final design for Stonehenge's business card. The one featured here is for Alexis Montgomery; however, each band member will have his own business card.

*The final design of Stonehenge's business card.*

# PROJECT 4: DESIGN LETTERHEAD FOR YOUR BAND

Approximate Completion Time: .5 hours

## OBJECTIVE:

To design letterhead stationery for your band

## PROJECT OVERVIEW:

As you begin the task of setting up and publicizing your band, you will be communicating with agents, tour operators, club owners, and potential employees. Having letterhead stationery will give your band a professional image as you send letters and other types of correspondence. In this project, you will use your desktop publishing skills to design your band's letterhead.

## GETTING TO KNOW WHAT YOU'RE DESIGNING:

A letterhead is a sheet of stationery with the name, address, logo and sometimes other relevant information of an organization printed at the top, bottom, left or right side. Letterhead is used to send business letters and other forms of correspondence and is created on standard size paper (8.5 x 11 inches).

## STRATEGIES AND DESIGN TIPS:

- Keep the look and design of your letterhead clean and simple so that the reader is not distracted.
- Obtain some examples of letterhead to use as a guide in your own design.
- Design the letterhead so that it fits within the first 2.5 inches of the top margin of the page.
- Stick to using one font (typeface) on the letterhead.
- So that it gets noticed, be sure that your logo is the largest element on the letterhead.
- Review the letterhead designed by Stonehenge in the "Spotlight on Stonehenge" section to get inspiration and ideas for designing your own. *Remember:* Use your own creativity and design skills. Do not copy Stonehenge's letterhead design.
- Use the "Concert Tour Document Planning Form" to plan the layout and design of your letterhead on paper first.

## INSTRUCTIONS:

1. Using your desktop publishing software, create a new document.
2. Save the document as "Letterhead" to the "Concert Tour DTP" folder.
3. Follow the Letterhead Page Setup Instructions provided on the next page.
4. Include the following on your letterhead:

REMEMBER TO PLAN YOUR DESIGN ON THE DOCUMENT PLANNING FORM FIRST!

- ☑ Your band's logo
- ☑ Your band's slogan or tagline (if you have created one)
- ☑ Contact information including your band's address, city, state, zip code, phone number, fax number, e-mail address, and Web site address
- ☑ A thin line to divide the letterhead region from the rest of the page (optional)

5. Format the size and placement of the text and other elements on the letterhead so that they are in proportion with each other and project a professional image.

   **Note:** *The text and other elements should be placed within the top 2.5 inch margin. Do not let your design fall below this area.*

6. Carefully proofread your work for accuracy, format, spelling, and grammar.
7. Resave the document.
8. Print a copy of the document.
9. Write your name and "Project 4 Letterhead" on the document.

# LETTERHEAD PAGE SETUP INSTRUCTIONS:

| | |
|---|---|
| **# of Pages:** | 1 |
| **Dimensions:** | 8.5 x 11 inches |
| **Margins:** | Top: 1.5 to 2.5 inches (depending on your design) |
| | Left, right, and bottom: .75 inches |
| **Orientation:** | Portrait |

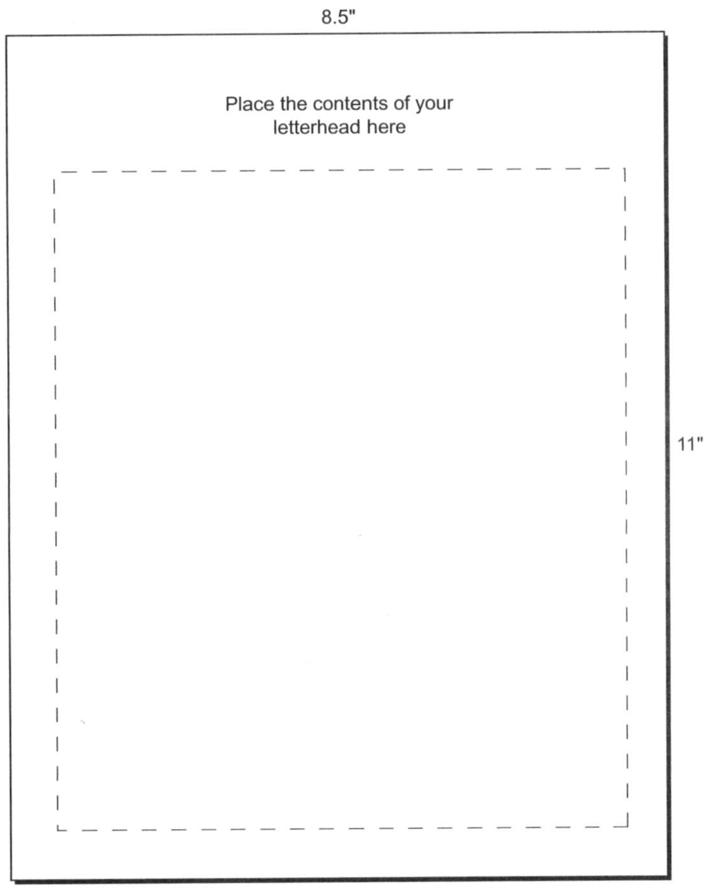

# About Stonehenge's Letterhead:

To create a cohesive, consistent, and professional design, Stonehenge mirrored the design of their business card to create their letterhead. Provided below is the final design for Stonehenge's letterhead. Notice the consistency, simplicity, and professionalism Stonehenge is beginning to establish in the design of their band's documents.

STONE HENGE

11 Grover Street · Sparta, MI 49345
Phone: 616.817.8624 · Fax: 616.817.5515
E-mail: info@stonehengeband.net
www.stonehengeband.net

*A Classic Blend of Classic Rock*

*The final design of Stonehenge's letterhead.*

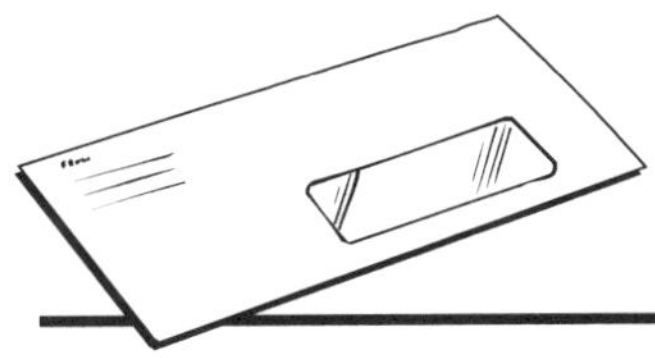

# PROJECT 5: DESIGN AN ENVELOPE FOR YOUR BAND

Approximate Completion Time: .5 hours

## OBJECTIVE:

To design an envelope for your band

## PROJECT OVERVIEW:

In this project, you will use your desktop publishing skills to design an envelope that coordinates with your band's letterhead created in Project 4. The envelope will complete the design of your band's stationery.

## GETTING TO KNOW WHAT YOU'RE DESIGNING:

An envelope is one of the most important documents a business uses, yet its design is often overlooked. An envelope is the first document that recipients see. The envelope is what makes the first impression for a business. Common elements found on an envelope are the company name, address, and sometimes Web site address located in the top left-hand corner and the recipient's address in the center. The standard size of a business envelope (also known as a #10 envelope) is 4.125 inches tall x 9.5 inches wide.

## STRATEGIES AND DESIGN TIPS:

- Model the design of your envelope to align with that of your letterhead and business card.
- Keep the design of your envelope simple.
- Obtain some examples of envelopes to use as a guide in your own design.
- Review the envelope designed by Stonehenge in the "Spotlight on Stonehenge" section to get inspiration and ideas for designing your own. *Remember*: Use your own creativity and design skills. Do not copy Stonehenge's envelope design.
- Use the "Concert Tour Document Planning Form" to plan the layout and design of your envelope on paper first.

## INSTRUCTIONS:

1. Using your desktop publishing software, create a new document.
2. Save the document as "Envelope" to the "Concert Tour DTP" folder.
3. Follow the Envelope Page Setup Instructions provided on the next page.
4. Include the following in the return address area on your envelope:

> ☑ Your band's logo
>
> ☑ Your band's slogan or tagline (if you have created one)
>
> ☑ Contact information including your band's address, city, state, zip code, and Web site address

REMEMBER TO PLAN YOUR DESIGN ON THE DOCUMENT PLANNING FORM FIRST!

5. Format the size and placement of the text and other elements on the envelope so that they are in proportion with each other and project a professional image.
6. Carefully proofread your work for accuracy, format, spelling, and grammar.
7. Resave the document.
8. Print a copy of the document.
9. Write your name and "Project 5 Envelope" on the document.

# ENVELOPE PAGE SETUP INSTRUCTIONS:

| | |
|---|---|
| **# of Pages:** | 1 |
| **Dimensions:** | 11 x 8.5 inches |
| **Margins:** | 0 inches on all sides |
| **Orientation:** | Landscape |
| **Optional Materials:** | #10 business-size envelope |
| **Other:** | Draw a rectangle that measures 9.5 inches wide by 4.125 inches tall. Place the rectangle in the center of the page. This rectangle represents the envelope on your page. Place the contents of the envelope within this rectangle. |
| **Suggested:** | Print the document on a real #10 business envelope |

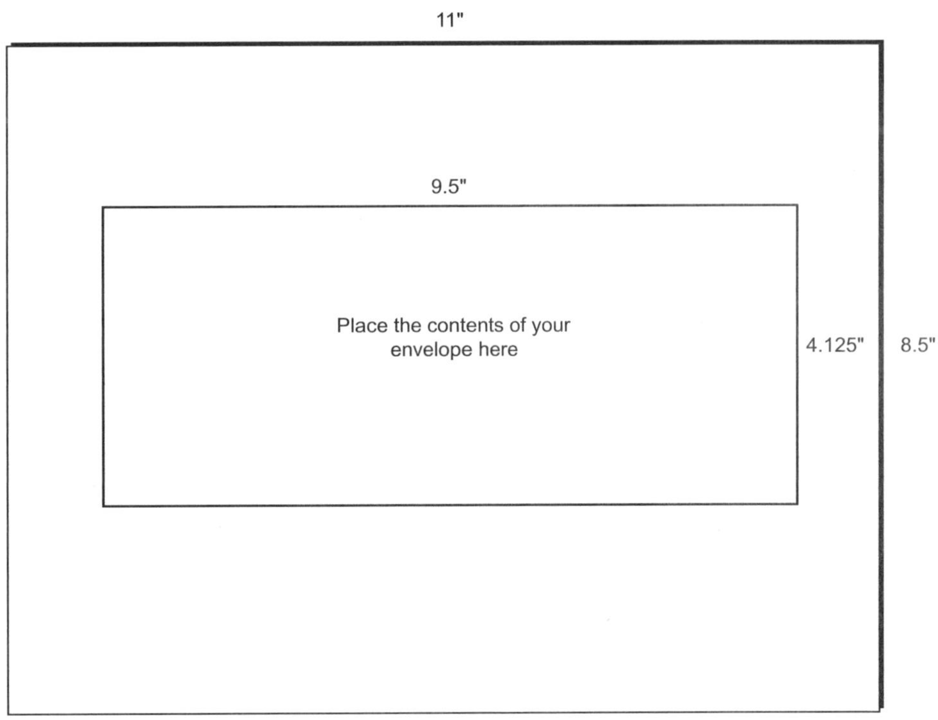

# About Stonehenge's Envelope:

In keeping with the design of their letterhead and business card, Stonehenge created the following envelope design for their band.

*The final design of Stonehenge's envelope.*

# PART 3: THE FREE CONCERT

CONCERT TOUR
DESKTOP PUBLISHER

## PROJECTS INCLUDED:

Project 6: Design a Concert Flyer
Project 7: Design a Concert T-shirt
Project 8: Design a Bumper Sticker for Your Band
Project 9: Design a Promotional Concert Frisbee

# PROJECT 6: DESIGN A CONCERT FLYER

Approximate Completion Time: 1 - 2 hours

## OBJECTIVE:

To design a flyer for your band's first concert

## PROJECT OVERVIEW:

It is time to generate some publicity about your newly formed band, so you decide to hold a free concert in your community's local park. The free concert flyer will hopefully get people to come and hear your band play. In this project, you will use your desktop publishing skills to design a concert flyer to help advertise the big event. The flyer will be posted around your school, inside of local businesses, and on telephone poles in your surrounding community.

## GETTING TO KNOW WHAT YOU'RE DESIGNING:

A flyer is used to communicate a simple message to an audience. It can take on a variety of formats and sizes. The design of a flyer can range from simple to complex. Flyers are used to announce events, advertise a product or service, or promote a cause. The primary objective of a flyer is to capture the reader's attention using minimal space.

## STRATEGIES AND DESIGN TIPS:

- Most readers view flyers as "light" reading material, so try to keep the word count to a minimum while still keeping the reader's attention.
- Use a maximum of three fonts (typefaces) throughout your flyer.
- Do not clutter the flyer with too many graphic images, as this will distract readers.
- Use a layout and design scheme that is easy to read. The most important information should be placed near the top and middle areas of the flyer.
- Obtain some examples of flyers placed throughout your school and/or community to use as a guide as you design your own.
- Consider using a digital camera to include photographs of each member of your band on your flyer.
- Review the flyer designed by Stonehenge in the "Spotlight on Stonehenge" section to get inspiration and ideas for designing your own. *Remember:* Use your own creativity and design skills. Do not copy Stonehenge's concert flyer design.
- Use the "Concert Tour Document Planning Form" to plan the layout and design of your flyer on paper first.

## INSTRUCTIONS:

1. Using your desktop publishing software, create a new document.
2. Save the document as "Flyer" to the "Concert Tour DTP" folder.
3. Follow the Concert Flyer Page Setup Instructions provided on the next page.
4. Include the following on your flyer:

**REMEMBER TO PLAN YOUR DESIGN ON THE DOCUMENT PLANNING FORM FIRST!**

☑ A simple-to-read, eye-catching headline
***Examples:*** "Free Concert Coming Soon!"
"Premiere Free Concert of <Your Band Name>"

☑ Your band's logo

☑ Your band's slogan or tagline (if you have created one)

☑ Information about the type of music your band plays

☑ The names of each member in your band (optional)

☑ A "Call to Action" which includes the date, time, and location of the concert

☑ Contact information including your band's address, city, state, zip code, phone number, fax number, e-mail and Web site address

☑ Additional text and/or graphic images that will help make the flyer achieve the objective of getting people to attend the concert

5. Format the size and placement of the text and other elements on the flyer so that they are in proportion with each other and project a professional image.
6. Carefully proofread your work for accuracy, format, spelling, and grammar.
7. Resave the document.
8. Print a copy of the document.
9. Write your name and "Project 6 Flyer" on the document.

# CONCERT FLYER PAGE SETUP INSTRUCTIONS:

| | |
|---|---|
| **# of Pages:** | 1 |
| **Dimensions:** | 8.5 x 11 inches |
| **Margins:** | .75 inches on all sides |
| **Orientation:** | Portrait |
| **Optional Materials:** | Colored paper |

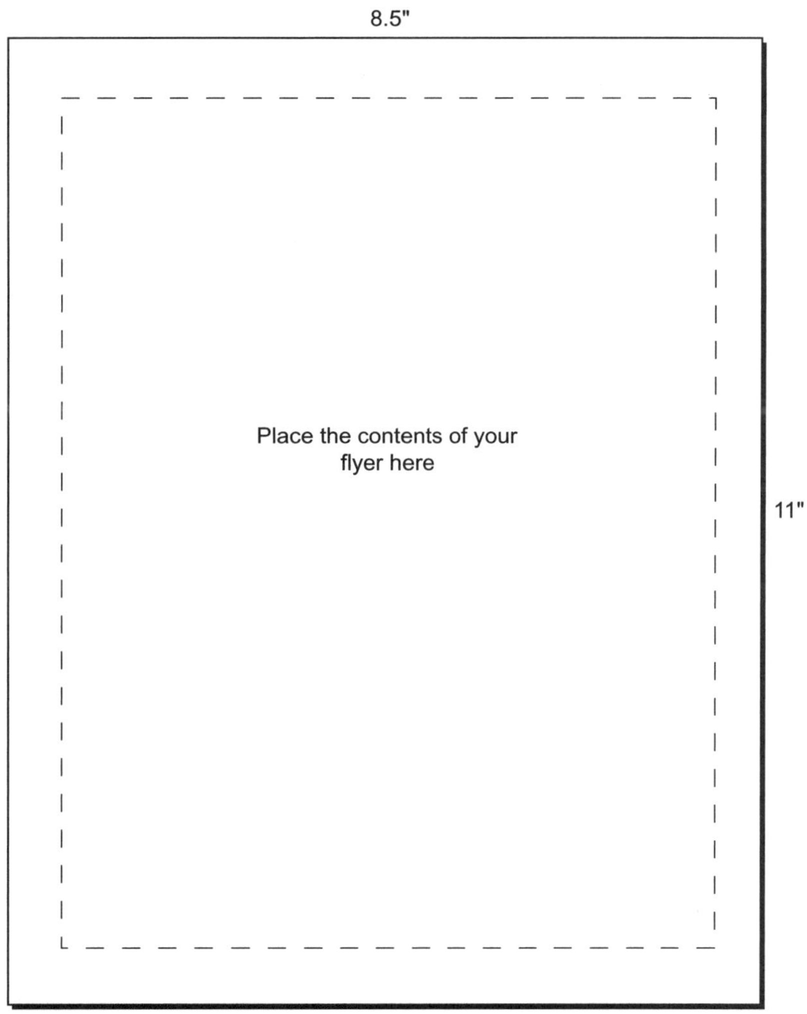

# About Stonehenge's Concert Flyer:

The members of Stonehenge were ecstatic about playing their first real concert. Stonehenge knew that in order to capture the attention of potential concertgoers and make a great first impression, they would need to create and design a well-written, eye-catching flyer. The band members agreed that the primary focus of the flyer would be that the concert was free. They also wanted to be sure to attract the right audience by highlighting the type of music they play as well.

After sketching several design schemes on paper first, Stonehenge created the flyer provided below to advertise their first concert.

*The final design of Stonehenge's concert flyer.*

# PROJECT 7: DESIGN A CONCERT T-SHIRT

Approximate Completion Time: .5 hours

## OBJECTIVE:

To design a concert T-shirt for your band to be sold at the free concert in the park

## PROJECT OVERVIEW:

Capitalizing on the free publicity you will be receiving from the free concert in the park, you are going to sell T-shirts at the concert. Your friends have agreed to sell the shirts at a booth that will be set up near the entrance to the concert. Hopefully, your band will generate some revenue from the sales to use for future marketing efforts. In this project, you will use your desktop publishing skills to design a concert T-shirt to sell at your free concert. After the design is complete, it will be screen printed onto real T-shirts that will be sold at the concert.

## GETTING TO KNOW WHAT YOU'RE DESIGNING:

T-shirts that include a design printed on them are referred to as "novelty T's." Novelty T-shirts offer businesses a walking form of free advertising. T-shirt designs take on many forms, shapes, and sizes--from simple text to detailed graphics. A novelty T-shirt can include text and/or graphics printed on the front, back, and even the sleeves.

## STRATEGIES AND DESIGN TIPS:

- If including a graphic image, be sure that it is large enough to be seen.
- If using a graphic image, keep it simple so that the viewer can tell what it is.
- Use a font (typeface) that is easy to read.
- Do not clutter the T-shirt design with too much text or too many graphic images. Keep it clean and simple.
- Make your band's logo the largest element on the T-shirt. *Remember*: The purpose of the T-shirt is to gain exposure of your band.
- Review the T-shirt designed by Stonehenge in the "Spotlight on Stonehenge" section to get inspiration and ideas for designing your own. Remember: Use your own creativity and design skills. Do not copy Stonehenge's T-shirt design.
- Use the "Concert Tour Document Planning Form" to plan the layout and design of your T-shirt on paper first.

## INSTRUCTIONS:

1. Using your desktop publishing software, create a new document.
2. Save the document as "T-shirt" to the "Concert Tour DTP" folder.
3. Follow the Concert T-shirt Page Setup Instructions provided on the next page.
4. Include the following on the front of the T-shirt (the back will be left blank):

REMEMBER TO PLAN YOUR DESIGN ON THE DOCUMENT PLANNING FORM FIRST!

- ☑ An eye-catching headline that captures the theme of the free concert in the park (optional)
- ☑ Your band's logo
  **Note:** *This should be the largest element on your T-shirt*
- ☑ Your band's slogan or tagline (optional)
- ☑ The date and location of the free concert
- ☑ The names and pictures of each member in your band (optional)
- ☑ Your band's Web site address (optional)
- ☑ Additional text and/or graphic images that will help make the T-shirt an attractive selling piece

5. Format the size and placement of the text and other elements on the T-shirt so that they are in proportion with each other and project a professional image.
6. Carefully proofread your work for accuracy, format, spelling, and grammar.
7. Resave the document.
8. Print a copy of the document.
9. Write your name and "Project 7 T-shirt" on the document.

# CONCERT T-SHIRT PAGE SETUP INSTRUCTIONS:

| | |
|---|---|
| **# of Pages:** | 1 |
| **Dimensions:** | 8.5 x 11 inches |
| **Margins:** | .75 inches on all sides |
| **Orientation:** | Portrait |
| **Optional Materials:** | Colored paper, T-shirt transfer paper |
| **Other:** | Place the contents of the T-shirt design inside a graphic image of a blank T-shirt (optional). |

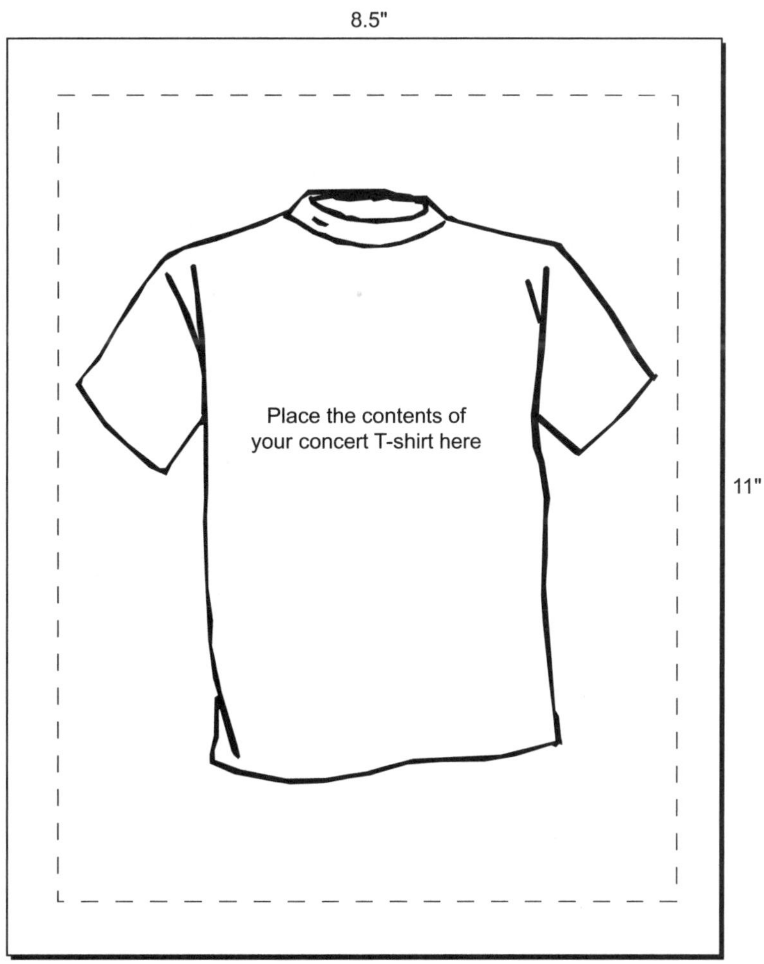

# About Stonehenge's Concert T-shirt:

Following the design scheme from their concert flyer, Stonehenge set out to create a T-shirt design that highlighted their band's name and logo. To create a bit of "mystery" for viewers, the band decided not to include their photos or names on the T-shirt. The end result was a crisp, clean T-shirt design that concertgoers would want to purchase. Here is the final design for Stonehenge's concert T-shirt.

*The final design of Stonehenge's concert T-shirt.*

# PROJECT 8: DESIGN A BUMPER STICKER FOR YOUR BAND

Approximate Completion Time: .5 hours

## OBJECTIVE:

To design a bumper sticker for your band to distribute at your free concert

## PROJECT OVERVIEW:

The free concert in the park is all about publicizing your new band. A great way to get the band's name out in public is to hand out free bumper stickers to people who attend the concert. In this project, you will use your desktop publishing skills to create a great looking bumper sticker that your fans can put on their cars to promote your band.

## GETTING TO KNOW WHAT YOU'RE DESIGNING:

A bumper sticker is a sticker bearing a printed message for display on a vehicle's bumper. Due to the fact that bumper stickers are placed on moving vehicles, they usually contain only one message. Yet, bumper stickers serve as a highly visible and effective marketing tool for businesses.

## STRATEGIES AND DESIGN TIPS:

- Use the Internet to search for examples of bumper stickers. Use the examples you obtain as a guide to design your own.
- Consider using a block style font (typeface) on your bumper sticker since it will be easy to read from a distance.
- Due to limited space, use only one graphic image (if any) on your bumper sticker.
- Maximize the readability of your bumper sticker by leaving plenty of white space.
- Use a horizontal (left to right) layout design on your bumper sticker.
- Be sure that your band's logo is the most prevalent element on your bumper sticker.
- Review the bumper sticker designed by Stonehenge in the "Spotlight on Stonehenge" section to get inspiration and ideas for designing your own. *Remember:* Use your own creativity and design skills. Do not copy Stonehenge's bumper sticker design.
- Use the "Concert Tour Document Planning Form" to plan the layout and design of your bumper sticker on paper first.

## INSTRUCTIONS:

1. Using your desktop publishing software, create a new document.
2. Save the document as "Bumper Sticker" to the "Concert Tour DTP" folder.
3. Follow the Bumper Sticker Page Setup Instructions provided on the next page.
4. Include the following on your bumper sticker:

REMEMBER TO PLAN YOUR DESIGN ON THE DOCUMENT PLANNING FORM FIRST!

- ☑ Your band's logo
- ☑ Your band's slogan or tagline (optional)
- ☑ A large headline that captures the eye of onlookers (optional)
- ☑ Your band's Web site address
- ☑ Additional text and/or one graphic image that will help to get the bumper sticker noticed

5. Format the size and placement of the text and other elements on the bumper sticker so that they are in proportion with each other and project a professional image.
6. Carefully proofread your work for accuracy, format, spelling, and grammar.
7. Resave the document.
8. Print a copy of the document.
9. Write your name and "Project 8 Bumper Sticker" on the document.

# BUMPER STICKER PAGE SETUP INSTRUCTIONS:

| | |
|---|---|
| **# of Pages:** | 1 |
| **Dimensions:** | 11 x 8.5 inches |
| **Margins:** | .25 inches on all sides |
| **Orientation:** | Landscape |
| **Optional Materials:** | Full-sheet laser or ink-jet compatible paper |
| **Other:** | Create a rectangle that measures 10.5 inches wide by 3 inches tall. Place the rectangle in the center of the page. Place the contents of the bumper sticker within this rectangle. |

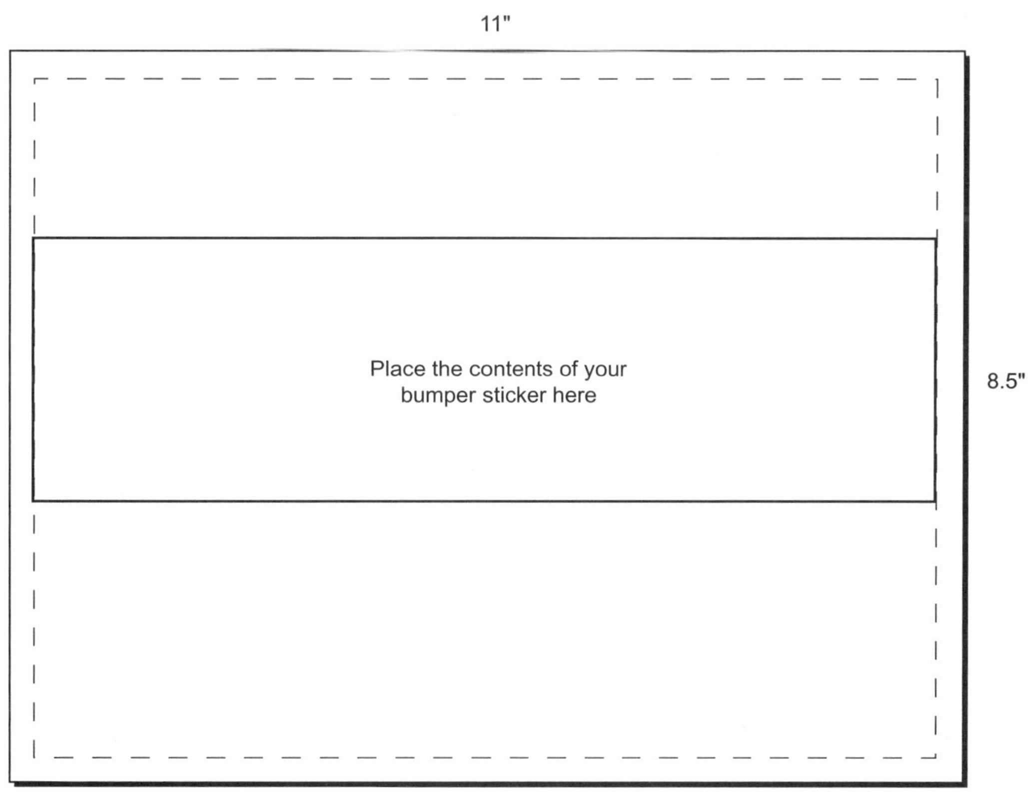

## About Stonehenge's Bumper Sticker:

Stonehenge had one goal with the design of their bumper sticker: To get the name of their band noticed. To accomplish this, Stonehenge used only their logo, Web site address, and a catchy headline on their bumper sticker. The final result was a design that they felt would be easily seen by onlookers. Stonehenge created the bumper sticker provided below to pass out at their free concert.

*The final design of Stonehenge's bumper sticker.*

# PROJECT 9: DESIGN A PROMOTIONAL CONCERT FRISBEE

Approximate Completion Time: .5 hours

## OBJECTIVE:

To create a promotional concert Frisbee design that will be distributed at your free concert in the park

## PROJECT OVERVIEW:

In addition to the free bumper stickers, you will also be distributing free miniature Frisbee souvenirs to the fans attending your free concert in the park. You and other band members will be randomly throwing out the Frisbees to the crowd during the concert. The Frisbees will serve a dual purpose at the concert. They will help to promote your band, and they will send the message that your band "likes to have fun" while performing. In this project, you will be using your desktop publishing skills to create the design that will be printed on the Frisbees.

## GETTING TO KNOW WHAT YOU'RE DESIGNING:

Just about everyone has played with a Frisbee. Frisbees are timeless toys that appeal to all ages. Businesses have used the Frisbee's popularity as a creative way to advertise their product or service by printing their company name, logo, and other information on it.

## STRATEGIES AND DESIGN TIPS:

- Use the Internet to search for examples of custom-printed Frisbees. Use the examples you obtain as a guide to design your own.
- Consider using a block style font (typeface) on your Frisbee as it will be easier to read.
- Think of an easily remembered "catch phrase" to put on the Frisbee.
- Experiment with placing text and/or graphic images along a curved path that matches the circle border as shown in the Concert Frisbee Page Setup Instructions.
- Be sure that your band's logo is the most prevalent element on your Frisbee.
- Create a Frisbee design that is fan-friendly; one that will make fans want to take the Frisbee home with them after the concert.
- Review the Frisbee designed by Stonehenge in the "Spotlight on Stonehenge" section to get inspiration and ideas for designing your own. *Remember*: Use your own creativity and design skills. Do not copy Stonehenge's Frisbee design.
- Use the "Concert Tour Document Planning Form" to plan the layout and design of your Frisbee on paper first.

## INSTRUCTIONS:

1. Using your desktop publishing software, create a new document.
2. Save the document as "Concert Frisbee" to the "Concert Tour DTP" folder.
3. Follow the Concert Frisbee Page Setup Instructions provided on the next page.
4. Include the following on your Frisbee:

**REMEMBER TO PLAN YOUR DESIGN ON THE DOCUMENT PLANNING FORM FIRST!**

- ☑ Your band's logo
- ☑ Your band's slogan or tagline (optional)
- ☑ A large headline or "catch phrase" that captures the attention of concertgoers (optional)
- ☑ Your band's contact information including address, city, state, zip code, phone number, fax number, e-mail and Web site address (optional)
- ☑ Your band's Web site address
- ☑ The names of each member in your band (optional)
- ☑ Additional text and/or graphic images that will help enhance the design and appearance of the Frisbee (Remember to make the Frisbee design "fun")

5. Format the size and placement of the text and other elements on the Frisbee so that they are in proportion with each other and project a professional, fun image.
6. Carefully proofread your work for accuracy, format, spelling, and grammar.
7. Resave the document.
8. Print a copy of the document.
9. Write your name and "Project 9 Frisbee" on the document.

# CONCERT FRISBEE PAGE SETUP INSTRUCTIONS:

| | |
|---|---|
| **# of Pages:** | 1 |
| **Dimensions:** | 8.5 x 11 inches |
| **Margins:** | .4 inches on all sides |
| **Orientation:** | Portrait |
| **Other:** | Draw a perfect circle border measuring 7.5 inches in diameter. Place this border in the center of the document. Place the contents of your Frisbee design within this border.<br>**Note:** *Do not place any design elements within .25 inches from the bordered circle (the Frisbee).* |
| **Optional Materials:** | Colored cardstock paper |

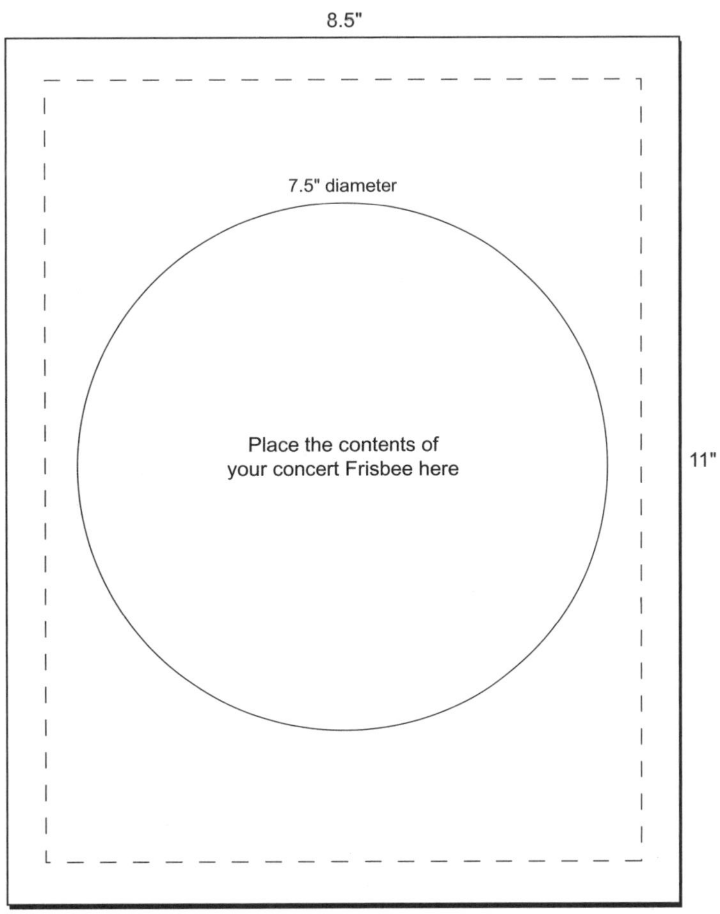

# About Stonehenge's Promotional Concert Frisbee:

Designing a Frisbee that promoted their band and added a spirit of "fun" to their free concert was a fun project for Stonehenge. After each band member submitted different Frisbee design ideas, Stonehenge decided to use the one shown below.

*The final design of Stonehenge's Frisbee.*

# PART 4: YOUR BAND GETS DISCOVERED

CONCERT TOUR
DESKTOP PUBLISHER

## PROJECTS INCLUDED:

Project 10: Design a CD Jewel Case
Project 11: Design a Poster for Your Band
Project 12: Design a Fan Club Newsletter
Project 13: Design a Fan Club Member Card

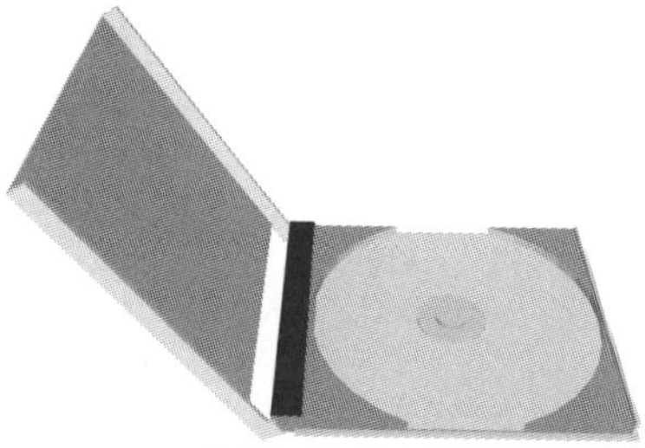

# PROJECT 10: DESIGN A CD JEWEL CASE

Approximate Completion Time: 1.5 - 3 hours

## OBJECTIVE:

To create a CD jewel case design for your band's first CD

## PROJECT OVERVIEW:

Since the signing of your new recording contract with Pinnacle Records, your band has been in meetings with music executives discussing the details about your band's first CD. The executives have asked your band to submit a design for the CD, including the title of the CD, a list of songs that will be included, and other details. In this project, you will use your desktop publishing skills to create the design of the front and back covers of your band's CD jewel case.

## GETTING TO KNOW WHAT YOU'RE DESIGNING:

Music CDs are packaged inside of a CD jewel case with printed paper inserts, also known as "tray cards." Common elements found on the cover and back of CD jewel case inserts are the band's name, logo, title of the CD, song list, copyright information, bar codes, band member names, titles, pictures, and other design elements that help attract the attention of the CD's target audience. The actual CD usually is a mirror image of the jewel case cover design.

## STRATEGIES AND DESIGN TIPS:

- Obtain some examples of music CD jewel cases. Use the examples you obtain as a guide to design your own.
- Experiment with different design ideas that will closely match the theme and title of your band's CD.
- Compile a list of possible song titles to use on the back of the CD jewel case.
- Consider using photos of each member in your band on the front and/or back of your CD jewel case design.
- Consider using framed borders to organize and separate different elements displayed on the CD jewel case.
- Review the CD jewel case designed by Stonehenge in the "Spotlight on Stonehenge" section to get inspiration and ideas for designing your own. *Remember*: Use your own creativity and design skills. Do not copy Stonehenge's CD jewel case design.
- Use the "Concert Tour Document Planning Form" to plan the layout and design of the front and back covers of your CD jewel case on paper first.

## INSTRUCTIONS:

1. Using your desktop publishing software, create a new document.
2. Save the document as "CD Jewel Case" to the "Concert Tour DTP" folder.
3. Follow the CD Jewel Case Page Setup Instructions provided on page 70.
4. Include the following on the **front cover** of your CD jewel case:

REMEMBER TO PLAN YOUR DESIGN ON THE DOCUMENT PLANNING FORM FIRST!

- ☑ The title of the CD
- ☑ Your band's logo
- ☑ Your band's slogan or tagline (optional)
- ☑ One or more graphic images that will help illustrate the title and theme of the CD
- ☑ A photograph of your band (optional)
- ☑ Additional text, graphics, and/or design elements that will help enhance the appearance of the CD cover

5. Include the following on the **back cover** of your CD jewel case:

REMEMBER TO PLAN YOUR DESIGN ON THE DOCUMENT PLANNING FORM FIRST!

- ☑ The title of the CD
- ☑ Your band's logo
- ☑ A list of song titles included on the CD (a minimum of ten songs is required); the song titles should correlate with the theme and title of the CD
  **Note:** *Song titles must be appropriate for classroom use.*
- ☑ Your band's contact information including address, city, state, zip code, e-mail and Web site address
- ☑ The names and titles of each member in your band (optional)
- ☑ Individual photos of each member in your band (optional)
- ☑ A UPC (Universal Product Code) barcode (to add realism to the CD)

*(continued)*

*(continued)*

- ☑ The following copyright information:

  © 20XX. All Rights Reserved. Pinnacle Recording Co. and <the name of your band>

- ☑ Additional text, graphics, and/or design elements that will help enhance the appearance of the CD cover

6. Format the size and placement of the text and other elements on the CD jewel case so that they are in proportion with each other and project a professional image.
7. Carefully proofread your work for accuracy, format, spelling and grammar.
8. Resave the document.
9. Print a copy of the document.
10. Write your name and "Project 10 CD Jewel Case" on the document.

# CD JEWEL CASE PAGE SETUP INSTRUCTIONS:

| | |
|---|---|
| **# of Pages:** | 1 |
| **Dimensions:** | 8.5 x 11 inches |
| **Margins:** | .4 inches on all sides |
| **Orientation:** | Portrait |
| **Optional Materials:** | Blank CD jewel case, cardstock paper |
| **Other:** | (see below) |

**FOR THE FRONT COVER OF THE CD JEWEL CASE:**
Create a bordered frame measuring 5 inches wide by 4.75 inches tall. Place this border in the center of the document near the top margin of the page (as shown in the diagram below). Place the contents of the front cover of the CD jewel case within this border

**FOR THE BACK COVER OF THE CD JEWEL CASE:**
Create a bordered frame measuring 5.5 inches wide by 4.75 inches tall. Place this border in the center of the document near the bottom margin of the page (as shown in the diagram below). Place the contents of the back cover of the CD jewel case within this border.

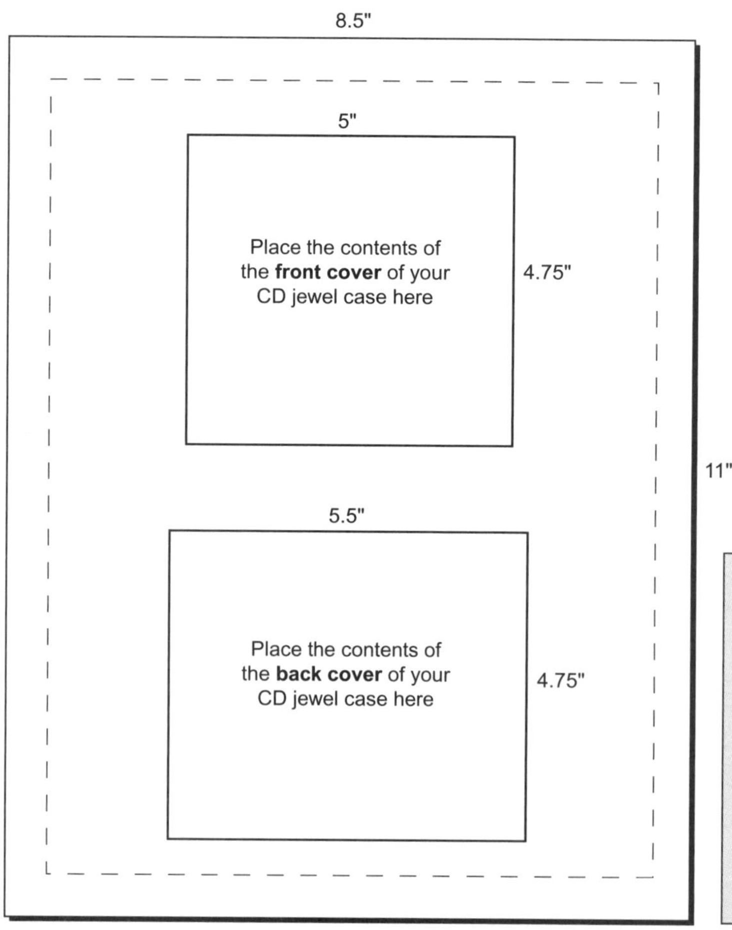


**SUGGESTED PRINTING INSTRUCTIONS:**
Print the document on card stock paper. Trim around the edges of the front and back covers of the CD jewel case. Insert the front and back covers into a blank CD jewel case.

# About Stonehenge's CD Jewel Case Design:

Stonehenge was ecstatic about creating the design for their first CD. Creating the song list was easy, but the band members spent a great deal of time deciding on the title and theme of their new CD.

After conducting several brainstorming sessions and surveying their existing fan-base, Stonehenge decided on the title of *Open Doors* for their new CD. The band then created a layout and design theme that correlated with their theme and title. Since this was Stonehenge's first CD, the members decided to include their names, photos, and titles on the front and back cover of the CD. Stonehenge's final CD jewel case design is provided below.

*The final design of Stonehenge's CD jewel case (front cover).*

*The final design of Stonehenge's CD jewel case (back cover).*

POSTER

# PROJECT 11: DESIGN A POSTER FOR YOUR BAND

Approximate Completion Time: 1 - 2 hours

## OBJECTIVE:

To design a poster that will be distributed at a "signing" party

## PROJECT OVERVIEW:

To celebrate the signing of your new recording contract, your band will be hosting a "signing" party at a banquet hall located in your community. Invited guests will include friends, family, and fans of your band. As a token of your band's appreciation, each guest will receive a poster, signed by each member in your band, at the "signing" party. In this project, you will be using your desktop publishing skills to design a poster that you will distribute at your signing party.

## GETTING TO KNOW WHAT YOU'RE DESIGNING:

A poster is a printed document that is used to illustrate and advertise an event, product, or cause. Posters usually contain a variety of graphic images, text, and other design elements to help communicate a message to an audience.

## STRATEGIES AND DESIGN TIPS:

- Obtain some examples of posters displayed around your community. Use the examples you obtain as a guide to design your own.
- An effective poster should be attractive, well organized and self-explanatory with the text and graphics linked to a specific target audience.
- The headline should be the largest element on the poster. It should be readable from at least five feet away.
- Organize different sections of your poster so they flow logically and support the main theme of the poster.
- Consider using bordered frames to help organize the information on your poster.
- Review the poster designed by Stonehenge in the "Spotlight on Stonehenge" section to get inspiration and ideas for designing your own. *Remember*: Use your own creativity and design skills. Do not copy Stonehenge's poster design.
- Use the "Concert Tour Document Planning Form" to plan the layout and design of your poster on paper first.

## INSTRUCTIONS:

1. Using your desktop publishing software, create a new document.
2. Save the document as "Poster" to the "Concert Tour DTP" folder.
3. Follow the Poster Page Setup Instructions provided on the next page.
4. Include the following on your poster:

REMEMBER TO PLAN YOUR DESIGN ON THE DOCUMENT PLANNING FORM FIRST!

- ☑ A large headline that captures the attention of the guests who will be attending the "signing" party
- ☑ Your band's logo
- ☑ Your band's slogan or tagline (optional)
- ☑ Your band's contact information including the address, city, state, zip code, phone number, fax number, e-mail and Web site address
- ☑ The names and titles of each member in your band
- ☑ A photograph of your band (optional)
- ☑ A brief summary of how your band got started; include a headline above the summary
- ☑ A thumbnail image of the CD jewel case front cover you designed in Project 10; include a picture caption underneath the image
- ☑ A message thanking your guests for attending the "signing" party
- ☑ To personalize the poster, include the date and location of the "signing" party
- ☑ Additional text and/or graphic images that will help enhance the design and appearance of the poster
- ☑ A border to frame all the elements on the poster

5. Format the size and placement of the text and other elements on the poster so that they are in proportion with each other and project a professional image.
6. Carefully proofread your work for accuracy, format, spelling, and grammar.
7. Resave the document.
8. Print a copy of the document.
9. Write your name and "Project 11 Poster" on the document.

# POSTER PAGE SETUP INSTRUCTIONS:

| | |
|---|---|
| **# of Pages:** | 1 |
| **Dimensions:** | 8.5 x 11 inches |
| **Margins:** | .5 inches on all sides |
| **Orientation:** | Portrait |
| **Optional Materials:** | Colored and/or glossy paper |
| **Other:** | Place a bordered frame aligned with the margins on the poster. Place the contents of your poster within this border. |

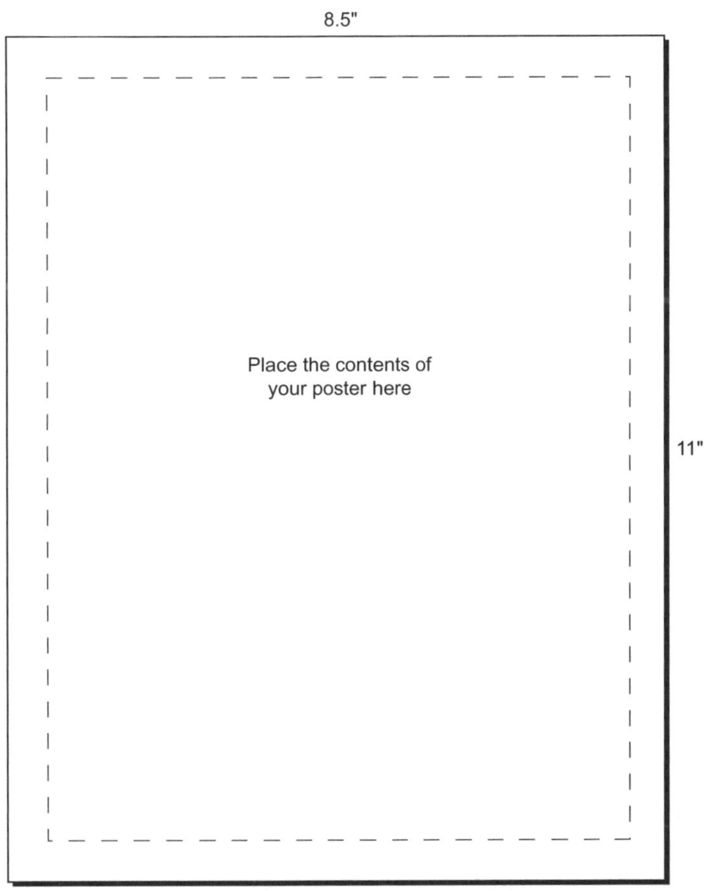


**SUGGESTED PRINTING AND FINISHING INSTRUCTIONS:**
Print the poster on colored and/or glossy paper. To add realism to this project, sign the poster using a pen or marker.

# About Stonehenge's Poster:

Stonehenge was excited about their "signing" party. The members of the band wanted to create a poster that their guests would be proud of. It was their first chance to deliver a sincere "thank you" to all of their fans and supporters. After several layout and design sessions, Stonehenge created the poster shown below.

*The final design of Stonehenge's poster.*

# PROJECT 12: DESIGN A FAN CLUB NEWSLETTER

Approximate Completion Time: 1.5 - 2 hours

## OBJECTIVE:

To design a newsletter to send to the members of your fan club

## PROJECT OVERVIEW:

During the free concert in the park, you collected a large number of names and addresses from new fans. The names and addresses have been entered into a database for your band to use to send out a newsletter. Staying in touch with your fans is important because it builds fan loyalty. Your band has decided to send out a quarterly one-page newsletter to keep everyone involved and updated. This will be sent to all fan club members and be available to fans at all concerts. Use your desktop publishing software to design a great looking newsletter.

## GETTING TO KNOW WHAT YOU'RE DESIGNING:

A newsletter is a periodically published document containing news and announcements about a subject or theme. The purpose of a newsletter is to provide highly specialized information to a targeted audience. Newsletters contain a masthead (also known as a nameplate) at the top which includes the title, volume number, month, and year. The articles and information in the body of a newsletter are usually placed in two or three columns and normally include relevant graphic images.

## STRATEGIES AND DESIGN TIPS:

- Obtain some examples of newsletters displayed around your community. Use the examples you obtain as a guide to design your own.
- An effective newsletter should be attractive, well organized, and self-explanatory with the text and graphics linked to a specific target audience.
- The masthead (also known as a nameplate) is the top portion of the newsletter that provides readers with the name, publication date, and other important information. The masthead should be the most prominent element of the newsletter, so take your time designing it.
- Organize different sections of your newsletter so they flow logically and support the title of the newsletter.
- Use a maximum of two or three different fonts (typefaces) throughout the newsletter.
- Review the newsletter designed by Stonehenge in the "Spotlight on Stonehenge" section to get inspiration and ideas for designing your own. *Remember:* Use your own creativity and design skills. Do not copy Stonehenge's newsletter design.
- Use the "Concert Tour Document Planning Form" to plan the layout and design of your newsletter on paper first.

## INSTRUCTIONS:

1. Using your desktop publishing software, create a new document.
2. Save the document as "Fan Club Newsletter" to the "Concert Tour DTP" folder.
3. Follow the Fan Club Newsletter Page Setup Instructions provided on the next page.
4. Include the following on your newsletter:

REMEMBER TO PLAN YOUR DESIGN ON THE DOCUMENT PLANNING FORM FIRST!

- ☑ A masthead design that includes a creative name for your newsletter and a publication date
  **Note:** *Your band's logo must be included in the masthead design.*
- ☑ A minimum of four articles (Each article should be given a headline)
  *Some suggested articles are:*
  - A summary of the free concert in the park
  - A description of your band's new CD
  - A summary about the signing party to celebrate your band's new recording contract
  - A brief biography of each member of your band
  - Information about how new fans can become members of your band's fan club
- ☑ Your band's contact information including the address, city, state, zip code, phone number, fax number, e-mail and Web site address
- ☑ A photograph of your band (optional)
- ☑ Additional text and/or graphic images that will help enhance the design and appearance of the newsletter

5. Format the size and placement of the text and other elements on the newsletter so that they are in proportion with each other and project a professional image.
6. Carefully proofread your work for accuracy, format, spelling, and grammar.
7. Resave the document.
8. Print a copy of the document.
9. Write your name and "Project 12 Fan Club Newsletter" on the document.

# FAN CLUB NEWSLETTER PAGE SETUP INSTRUCTIONS:

**# of Pages:** 1

**Dimensions:** 8.5 x 11 inches

**Margins:** .5 inches on all sides

**Orientation:** Portrait

**Optional Materials:** Colored cardstock paper

**Other:** **Step 1:** Place a horizontal guide at 2.5 inches. Place the masthead of the newsletter above this guide, but do not place any contents above the top margin guide.

**Step 2:** Use page or column guides to divide the page into two equal columns. Leave a .25 inch gutter space between the columns. Place the contents of the body of the newsletter within these columns. **Note:** *Do not place any contents inside the .25 inch gutter space (see the page setup illustration below for more assistance).*

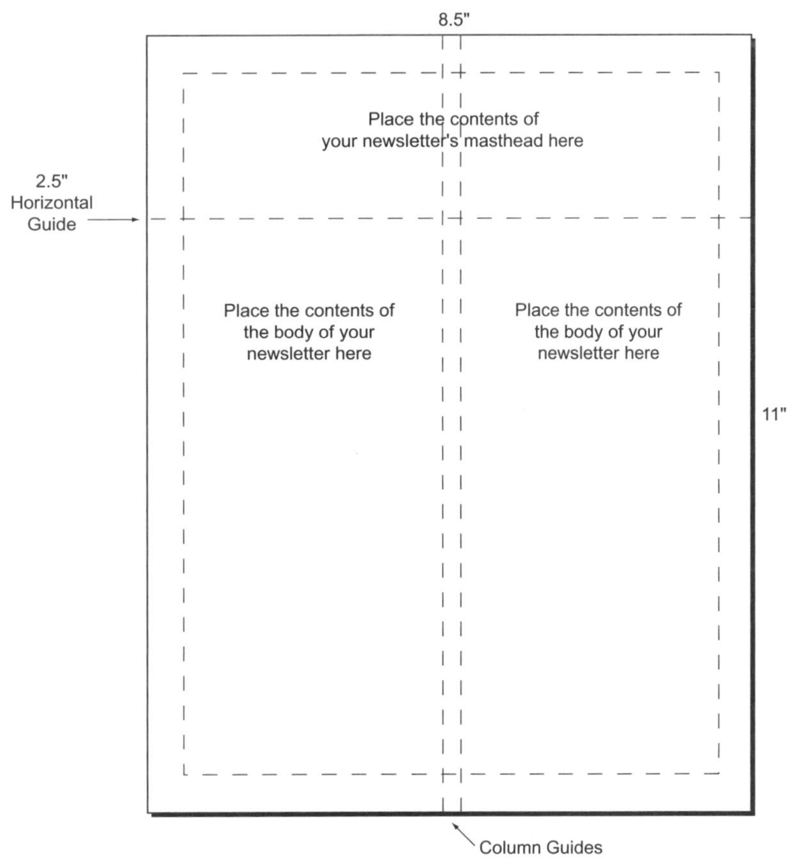

# About Stonehenge's Fan Club Newsletter:

Loyal fans should be rewarded. Stonehenge's newsletter will let the band stay in touch and up-to-date with fans all over the country. Here is the final design for Stonehenge's fan club newsletter.

## The Papered Slate

A Classic Blend of Classic Rock

*The Official Newsletter of the Stonehenge Band* — *July 2008, Issue 1*

### Rockin' at Roger's Park

On Friday, May 23, 2008, Stonehenge hit the stage like they had been in the music business for decades. Loyal Stonehenge fans were rockin' out for over three hours at Roger's Park in Sparta, MI. The energy on stage was purely magical and the fans left cheering for more. Even though the concert was free, some fans were quoted saying they would have paid hundreds to rock out at Stonehenge's debut concert. Alexis Montgomery, lead singer, said "Words cannot describe the atmosphere at Roger's Park. Everything went off better than we had planned, and we are psyched to hit the road for our Summer Concert Tour."

The band opened with "Salisbury Plain" from their *Open Doors* CD followed by "Now Is The Time" and "One Gem." But it wasn't until "Rainy Days" that lead guitarist Mitch Mason realized that he was actually playing for thousands of screaming fans. "This concert was surreal; I just can't describe how I feel." Stonehenge held out for ten minutes backstage before they came out for the encore song "Good Stuff." This song was a smash hit last year and it was exactly how the fans wanted to end the incredible night at Roger's Park.

### Stonehenge Celebrates Recording Contract

Stonehenge recently signed a recording contract with Pinnacle Records. After several months of ironing out the details, a representative for the band said that all parties involved are looking forward to a long and profitable relationship. Members of the band are elated that their Summer Concert Tour kicks off in late May, and they are ready to rock out with their fans. After their ten tour dates, they are planning to hit the studio to begin working on their sophomore CD.

### *Open Doors*
### *Stonehenge's Breakout CD Hits the Streets!*

Stonehenge spent many long nights in the studio recording for their debut CD *Open Doors*. All of their hard work paid off because it hit the charts at number eight its first week of release. Members of the band felt that creating the song titles was the easy part; deciding on the title and theme was where they struggled.

After holding several brainstorming sessions and surveying their fans, Stonehenge decided on *Open Doors* for their title. They felt this title best described the opportunities for their future. Having several doors open and seizing the moment to take advantage of the possibilities is why they are where they are today.

### How It All Started...

Several high school classmates attending Sparta High School in Sparta, Michigan formed the band Stonehenge in November 2007. Alexis Montgomery, the band's lead singer and side guitarist, wanted to take her talents to the stage, so she solicited musically talented students to try out to be in her band. After surveying more than 30 prospective band members, Stonehenge was formed when Alexis acquired three classmates to enlist in the band. They are Mitch Mason (lead guitarist), Corey Hill (drums, bongos), and Kyle Wilson (bass). You can find out more about each member in our next issue.

**11 Grover Street · Sparta, MI · 49345 · Phone: 616.817.8624**
**E-mail: info@stonehengeband.net · www.stonehengeband.net**

*The final design of Stonehenge's fan club newsletter.*

# PROJECT 13: DESIGN A FAN CLUB MEMBER CARD

Approximate Completion Time: .5 - 1 hour

## OBJECTIVE:

To design a membership card for your band's new fan club

## PROJECT OVERVIEW:

Since your band's big concert in the park and the "signing" party, fan response has been overwhelming. People in your hometown have even started a fan club. The new members have contacted you in hopes that you will design a membership card for the fan club. You can't turn them down. Use your desktop publishing software to design a member card they will be proud of.

## GETTING TO KNOW WHAT YOU'RE DESIGNING:

A membership card is a card certifying membership in an organization. A person will normally receive a member card after joining a club. The card will usually include the name of the member, the chapter, member number, and date of acceptance.

## STRATEGIES AND DESIGN TIPS:

- Obtain some samples of membership cards to use as a guide in designing your own. Some examples to obtain include health club, airline frequent flyer, and wholesale club membership cards.
- Avoid cluttering your fan club member card, and allow for plenty of white space to maximize readability.
- The overall look and feel of your fan club member card should match the style and design of your band's logo.
- Use a maximum of one or two fonts (typefaces) on your member card.
- Use a font (typeface) that is easy to read.
- Be sure that your band's logo is the most prevalent element on your fan club member card.
- Review the fan club member card designed by Stonehenge in the "Spotlight on Stonehenge" section to get inspiration and ideas for designing your own. *Remember*: Use your own creativity and design skills. Do not copy Stonehenge's fan club member card design.
- Use the "Concert Tour Document Planning Form" to plan the layout and design of your fan club member card on paper first.

## INSTRUCTIONS:

1. Using your desktop publishing software, create a new document.
2. Save the document as "Fan Club Member Card" to the "Concert Tour DTP" folder.
3. Follow the Fan Club Member Card Page Setup Instructions provided on the next page.
4. Include the following on your fan club member card:

**REMEMBER TO PLAN YOUR DESIGN ON THE DOCUMENT PLANNING FORM FIRST!**

- ☑ A headline title that identifies the card
  **Example:** *"Official Fan Club Member Card"*
- ☑ Your band's logo
- ☑ Your band's contact information including the address, city, state, zip code, phone number, fax number, Web site and e-mail address
- ☑ The month and year the card expires
- ☑ The following text:
  *"This is your official <your band's name> Fan Club Membership card. Present this card to get discounts and special offers on band merchandise and tickets. Thank you for your continued support of our band. We look forward to seeing you in the crowd."*
- ☑ A place for the fan club member to sign his or her name
- ☑ Additional text and/or graphic images that will help enhance the design and appearance of the fan club member card

5. Format the size and placement of the text and other elements on the fan club member card so that they are in proportion with each other and project a professional image.
6. Carefully proofread your work for accuracy, format, spelling, and grammar.
7. Resave the document.
8. Print a copy of the document.
9. Write your name and "Project 13 Fan Club Member Card" on the document.

# FAN CLUB MEMBER CARD PAGE SETUP INSTRUCTIONS:

| | |
|---|---|
| **# of Pages:** | 1 |
| **Dimensions:** | 8.5 x 11 inches |
| **Margins:** | 1 inch on all sides |
| **Orientation:** | Portrait |
| **Optional Materials:** | Colored cardstock paper |
| **Other:** | Using the rectangle tool in your desktop publishing software, draw a rectangle that measures 5 inches wide by 4 inches tall. Place the rectangle in the center of the page. Place the contents of the fan club member card within this rectangle. |

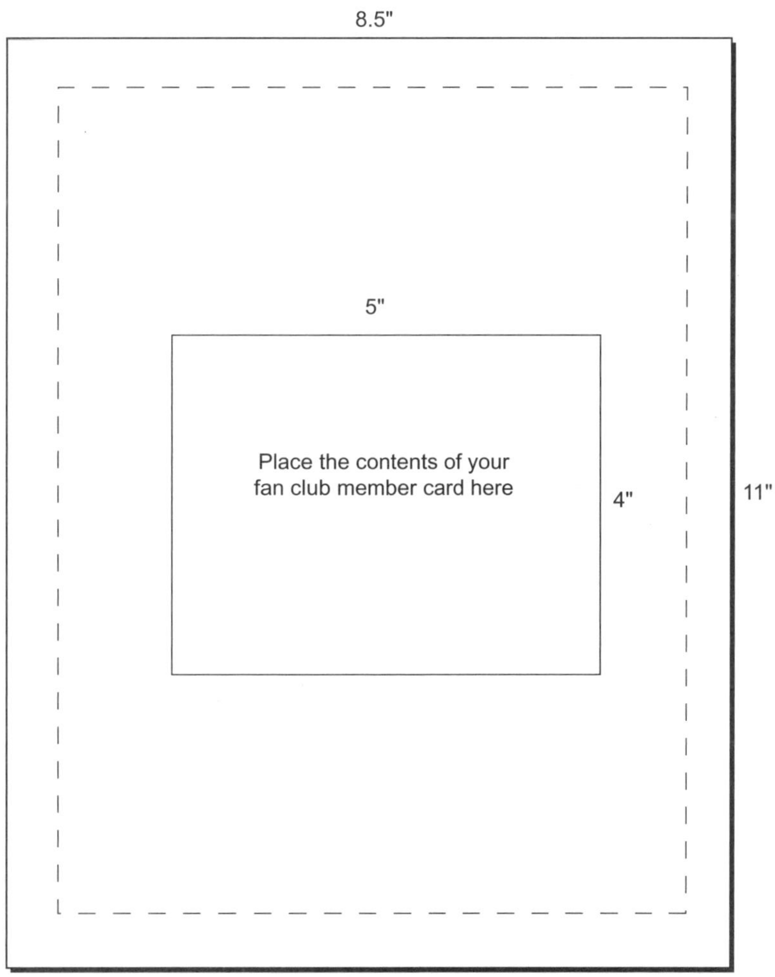

# About Stonehenge's Fan Club Member Card:

Now that the band is really taking off, the fan club members are increasing every day. Here is the final design for Stonehenge's fan club member card.

*The final design of Stonehenge's fan club member card.*

# PART 5: YOUR BAND GOES ON TOUR

CONCERT TOUR
DESKTOP PUBLISHER

## PROJECTS INCLUDED:

Project 14: Design a Three-Panel Brochure
Project 15: Design a Concert Ticket
Project 16: Design a Billboard Advertisement

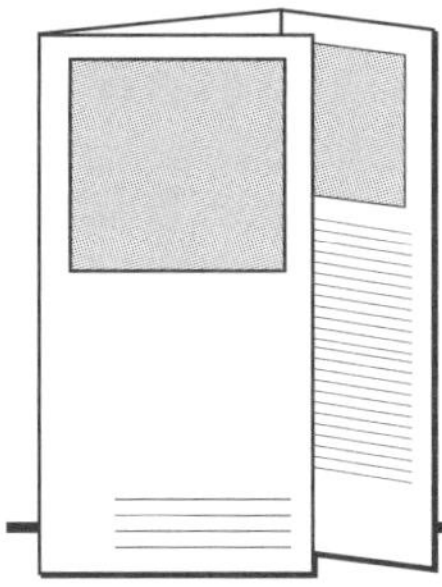

# PROJECT 14: DESIGN A THREE-PANEL BROCHURE

Approximate Completion Time: 2 - 3 hours

## OBJECTIVE:

To design a three-panel brochure about your band

## PROJECT OVERVIEW:

Traveling from town-to-town will be exciting. In each new town that you visit, members of the local media will want information about the band. How did the band start, what is the background of the members, concert dates, CD information, or how to buy band merchandise. A brochure is the perfect way to give them the answers to the questions they will ask. Use your desktop publishing software to design the perfect brochure for the band.

## GETTING TO KNOW WHAT YOU'RE DESIGNING:

A brochure is a small pamphlet, often containing promotional material or product information. Brochures are usually folded into two, three, or four panels. Brochures are popular because they are relatively small when folded and take up less desk or file space. And, because brochures are two-sided documents, they can communicate a large amount of information in a relatively small amount of space.

## STRATEGIES AND DESIGN TIPS:

- Use concise, clear wording to promote your band in your brochure.
- Be sure that your band's logo is the most prevalent element on the cover of your brochure.
- Use bulleted and/or numbered items, decorative borders, shaded areas, and graphic images to make your message easy to read and interesting to look at.
- Avoid cluttering your brochure by leaving enough white space around your text.
- Use a maximum of one or two fonts (typefaces) in your brochure.
- Use a sufficient ratio of graphic images to the amount of text.
- Review the brochure designed by Stonehenge in the "Spotlight on Stonehenge" section to get inspiration and ideas for designing your own. *Remember*: Use your own creativity and design skills. Do not copy Stonehenge's brochure design.
- Use the "Concert Tour Document Planning Form" to plan the layout and design of your brochure on paper first.

## INSTRUCTIONS:

1. Using your desktop publishing software, create a new document.
2. Save the document as "Brochure" to the "Concert Tour DTP" folder.
3. Follow the Three-Panel Brochure Page Setup Instructions provided on page 90.
4. Include the following on the **outside right panel (front cover)** of your brochure:

REMEMBER TO PLAN YOUR DESIGN ON THE DOCUMENT PLANNING FORM FIRST!

- ☑ A title for the brochure
- ☑ Your band's logo
- ☑ Additional text and/or graphic images that will help enhance the design and appearance of the outside right panel of the brochure

5. Include the following on the **outside middle panel (back cover)** of your brochure:

- ☑ Your band's contact information including the address, city, state, zip code, phone number, fax number, e-mail and Web site address
- ☑ Additional text and/or graphic images that will help enhance the design and appearance of the outside middle panel of the brochure

6. Include the following on the **outside left panel (inside cover)** of your brochure:

- ☑ An article that provides readers with information about how your band got started, how you were discoverd, and any additional information you would like readers to know
- ☑ Additional text and/or graphic images that will help enhance the design and appearance of the outside left panel of the brochure

7. Include the following on the **inside left panel** of your brochure:

> ☑ A brief biography about each member of your band
>
> ☑ A photograph of each member of your band (optional)
>
> ☑ Additional text and/or graphic images that will help enhance the design and appearance of the inside left panel of the brochure

8. Include the following on the **inside middle and right panels** of your brochure:

> ☑ A tour schedule for your band that includes a minimum of ten cities where your band will be performing concerts. The schedule should include the following columns, in the order shown:
>
> **Date** **Venue** **City, State** **Time**
>
> ☑ Information about how readers can purchase concert tickets to your band's concerts
>
> ☑ Additional text and/or graphic images that will help enhance the design and appearance of the inside middle and right panels of the brochure

9. Format the size and placement of the text and other elements on all six panels of the brochure so that they are in proportion with each other and project a professional image.
10. Carefully proofread your work for accuracy, format, spelling, and grammar.
11. Resave the document.
12. Print a copy of the document.
13. Write your name and "Project 14 Three-Panel Brochure" on the document.

# THREE-PANEL BROCHURE PAGE SETUP INSTRUCTIONS:

| | |
|---|---|
| **# of Pages:** | 2 |
| **Dimensions:** | 11 x 8.5 inches |
| **Margins:** | .25 inches on all sides |
| **Orientation:** | Landscape |
| **Optional Materials:** | Colored paper |
| **Other:** | Use page or column guides to divide both pages into three equal columns (panels). Leave a .5 inch gutter space between each column to allow for folding. **Note:** *Do not place any text or graphic images inside the gutter space. See the illustration below for more assistance.* |

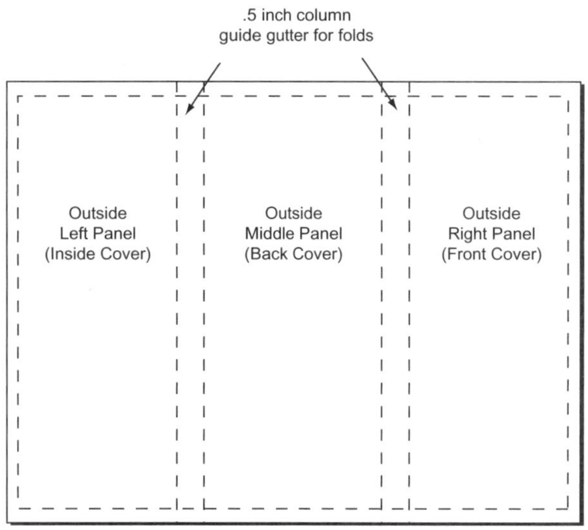


Page 1 (Side 1)

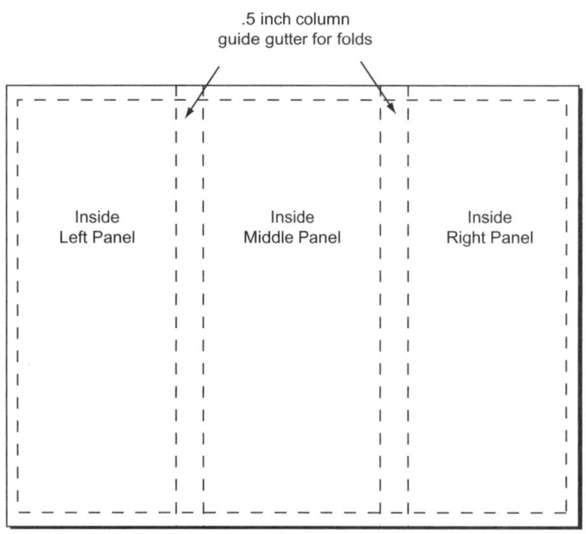


Page 2 (Side 2)

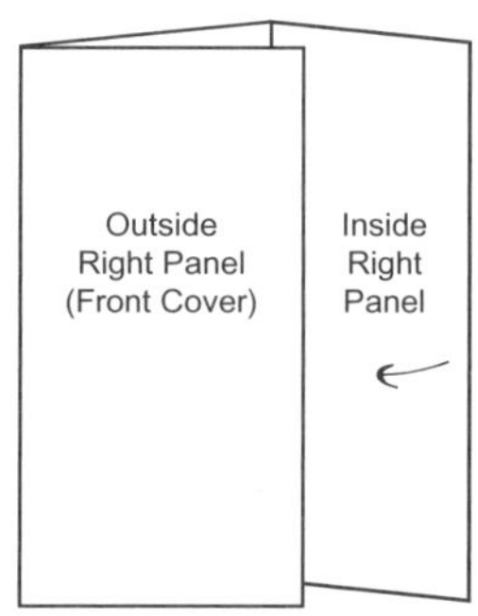


When folded, the finished brochure should look like this.

## PRINTING INSTRUCTIONS:

Print the brochure back-to-back (double-sided) or print both sides separately and staple them together.

# About Stonehenge's Three-Panel Brochure:

This brochure will tell fans everything they need to know about Stonehenge. Here is the final design for the band's brochure.

*Side 1 of the final design of Stonehenge's three-panel brochure (see the next page to view side 2).*

## Meet The Band...

**Alexis Montgomery** *(lead singer, side guitarist)*, is 17 years old. Born in Lansing, MI, to Jon and Allison Montgomery, Alexis has studied music most of her life. Her mom teaches vocal lessons and is a professor in the music department at a local community college. Alexis has two younger sisters and a black lab named Isaac. She will celebrate her 18th birthday with her band performing at Madison Square Garden on July 2, 2008. Besides music, Alexis loves to cook and watch the Cooking Channel in her spare time. Her best friend is her mom, and her favorite color is black because it matches everything.

**Mitch Mason** is the lead guitarist for Stonehenge and is 17 years old. He was born in Sparta, MI, to Mitchell and Suzanne Mason. Mitch is an only child and loves his two dogs Mutt and Jeff. In his spare time, Mitch skateboards and hangs out with his friends. He learned how to play guitar when he was ten years old, and he never really liked school because he thought it took away from practicing the guitar. He now realizes how important school is and regrets not studying when he needed to. He plans to attend college and major in public relations.

**Corey Hill** is the drummer for Stonehenge. He was born in Chicago, Illinois, and is 17 years old. He moved to Michigan when he was 15 and the first friend he met was Kyle Wilson. He is the youngest of three brothers and spends a lot of time writing for the band. As a Chicago native, his favorite baseball team is the Chicago White Sox. He loves pepperoni pizza and science fiction movies.

The youngest member of the band is 16-year-old **Kyle Wilson**. Kyle is the bass player for the band and was born and raised in Sparta, Michigan. He lives at home with his parents and brother, James. For fun, Kyle loves beating his brother at Playstation. He hopes to someday study computer animation and start his own company.

## Stonehenge Announces Ten City Summer Concert Tour '08

| Date | Venue | City/State | Time |
|---|---|---|---|
| May 30, 2008 | Wrigley Field | Chicago, IL | 8:00 pm |
| June 6, 2008 | HSBC Arena | Buffalo, NY | 8:00 pm |
| June 9, 2008 | Mellon Arena | Pittsburgh, PA | 7:00 pm |
| June 11, 2008 | TD Banknorth Garden | Boston, MA | 8:00 pm |
| June 28, 2008 | Times Union Center | Albany, NY | 7:30 pm |
| July 2, 2008 | Madison Square Garden | New York, NY | 8:00 pm |
| July 10, 2008 | Giants Stadium | East Rutherford, NJ | 7:00 pm |
| July 15, 2008 | Hartford Civic Center | Hartford, CT | 8:00 pm |
| July 21, 2008 | Wachovia Center | Philadelphia, PA | 7:00 pm |
| July 28, 2008 | Quicken Loan Arena | Cleveland, OH | 7:30 pm |

Tickets may be purchased at 1-888-NEW-BAND or online at www.stonehengeband.net

*Side 2 of the final design of Stonehenge's three-panel brochure.*

# PROJECT 15: DESIGN A CONCERT TICKET

Approximate Completion Time: .5 - 1 hour

## OBJECTIVE:

To design a ticket for the band's concert tour

## PROJECT OVERVIEW:

Even though your first concert in the park was free, the next one won't be. Create a ticket design that you can use when people start actually paying to see the band play. Use your desktop publishing software to design the ticket that will be used on your upcoming tour.

## GETTING TO KNOW WHAT YOU'RE DESIGNING:

A ticket is a form stating that the holder is entitled to enter a specific event, on a specific date, at a specific time. It will also state where that person's seat at the event is by section, row, and seat. Most tickets have a tear-off stub with the date and ticket number on it.

## STRATEGIES AND DESIGN TIPS:

- Consider different events or group activities an admission ticket would be used for. As a guide in designing your own, obtain some ticket stubs to events that you have gone to. Possibilities include school plays, sporting events, fundraising dinners, etc.
- Concert tickets present a lot of information in a small space. Utilize the space of your concert ticket to include only important information needed to attend the event, such as the name of the event, the date, the time, seat location, venue location, etc.
- Use a font (typeface) on your concert ticket that is easy to read.
- Review the concert ticket designed by Stonehenge in the "Spotlight on Stonehenge" section to get inspiration and ideas for designing your own. *Remember*: Use your own creativity and design skills. Do not copy Stonehenge's concert ticket.
- Use the "Concert Tour Document Planning Form" to plan the layout and design of your concert ticket on paper first.

## INSTRUCTIONS:

1. Using your desktop publishing software, create a new document.
2. Save the document as "Concert Ticket" to the "Concert Tour DTP" folder.
3. Follow the Concert Ticket Page Setup Instructions provided on the next page.
4. Include the following on your concert ticket:

REMEMBER TO PLAN YOUR DESIGN ON THE DOCUMENT PLANNING FORM FIRST!

- ☑ The name of your band
- ☑ The title or theme of the concert
- ☑ The name of the venue (where the concert is being held)
- ☑ The address, city, and state of the venue
- ☑ The ticket price
- ☑ A tear-off section that includes the ticket number, section, row, and seat number of the ticket
  **Hint**: *Use a dashed line to separate the tear-off part of the ticket*
- ☑ The date of the concert (day, month, and year)
- ☑ The time of the concert
- ☑ Additional text and/or graphic images that will help enhance the design and appearance of the concert ticket

5. Format the size and placement of the text and other elements on the concert ticket so that they are in proportion with each other and project a professional image.
6. Carefully proofread your work for accuracy, format, spelling, and grammar.
7. Resave the document.
8. Print a copy of the document.
9. Write your name and "Project 15 Concert Ticket" on the document.

# CONCERT TICKET PAGE SETUP INSTRUCTIONS:

| | |
|---|---|
| **# of Pages:** | 1 |
| **Dimensions:** | 8.5 x 11 inches |
| **Margins:** | 1 inch on all sides |
| **Orientation:** | Portrait |
| **Optional Materials:** | Colored cardstock paper |
| **Other:** | Draw a rectangle that measures 4.25 inches wide by 2.25 inches tall. Place the rectangle in the center of the page. Place the contents of the concert ticket within this rectangle. |

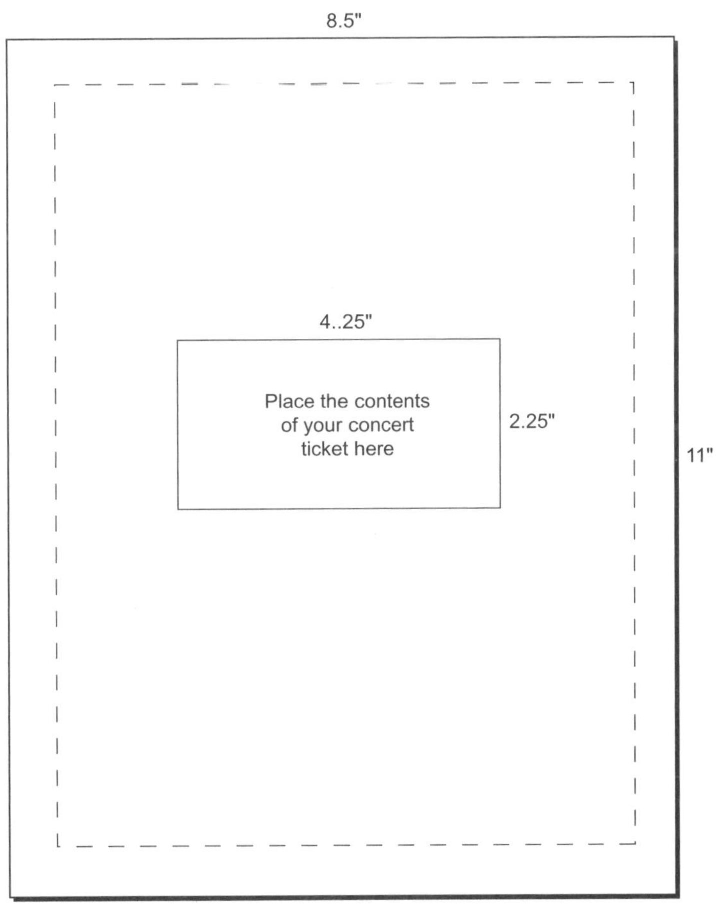

# About Stonehenge's Concert Ticket:

This ticket looks so good that Stonehenge fans will definitely keep it for their scrapbooks. Here is the final design for the band's concert ticket.

*The final design of Stonehenge's concert ticket.*

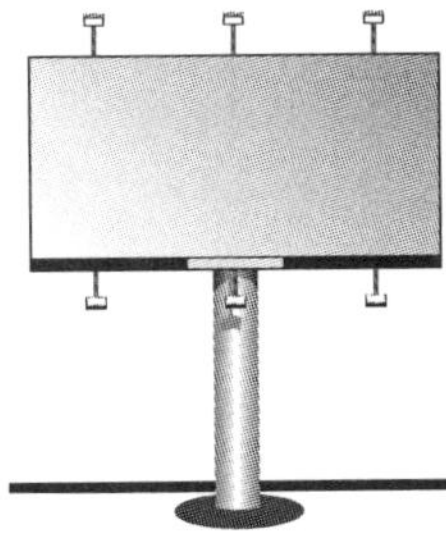

# PROJECT 16: DESIGN A BILLBOARD ADVERTISEMENT

Approximate Completion Time: 1 - 2 hours

## OBJECTIVE:

To create a billboard advertisement to promote your concert tour

## PROJECT OVERVIEW:

With your concert tour schedule in place, the next step before you take the stage nationally is to attract more fans to attend your band's concerts. To accomplish this, you will design a billboard advertisement. The advertisement will be strategically placed throughout the country in high traffic areas in the cities in which your band will be performing. The design of the billboard ad will be identical, except that the venue, and date of the concert will be changed accordingly. In this project, you will use your desktop publishing skills to create and design an eye-catching billboard advertisement that will bring a host of concertgoers to your national tour.

## GETTING TO KNOW WHAT YOU'RE DESIGNING:

A billboard is a panel for the display of advertisements in public places, such as alongside highways or on the sides of buildings. The advertiser's message is posted directly on the billboard panel.

## STRATEGIES AND DESIGN TIPS:

- Since a billboard is a "quick-read" form of advertising, you must grab the reader's attention with an easy-to-read dominant message.
- Your message and band logo should be the two most prominent elements on the billboard.
- Other important information should be in proportion with all elements.
- Use a maximum of one or two fonts (typefaces) on your billboard.
- Use a font (typeface) that is easy to read.
- The overall look of your billboard should match the image of your band.
- Review the billboard advertisement designed by Stonehenge in the "Spotlight on Stonehenge" section to get inspiration and ideas for designing your own. *Remember*: Use your own creativity and design skills. Do not copy Stonehenge's billboard advertisement design.
- Use the "Concert Tour Document Planning Form" to plan the layout and design of your billboard advertisement on paper first.

# Part 5, Project 16: Design a Billboard Advertisement

## INSTRUCTIONS:

1. Using your desktop publishing software, create a new document.
2. Save the document as "Billboard Ad" to the "Concert Tour DTP" folder.
3. Follow the Billboard Advertisement Page Setup Instructions provided on the next page.
4. Include the following on your billboard advertisement:

**REMEMBER TO PLAN YOUR DESIGN ON THE DOCUMENT PLANNING FORM FIRST!**

- ☑ A large headline that will capture the attention of onlookers
- ☑ The title or theme of the concert
- ☑ Your band's logo
- ☑ The name of the venue (where the concert will be held)
- ☑ The address, city, and state of the venue
- ☑ The date of the concert (day, month, and year)
- ☑ The time of the concert
- ☑ A call to action (information on how onlookers can purchase tickets)
- ☑ Additional text and/or graphic images that will help enhance the design and appearance of the billboard advertisement

5. Format the size and placement of the text and other elements on the billboard advertisement so that they are in proportion with each other and project a professional image.
6. Carefully proofread your work for accuracy, format, spelling, and grammar.
7. Resave the document.
8. Print a copy of the document.
9. Write your name and "Project 16 Billboard Ad" on the document.

# BILLBOARD ADVERTISEMENT PAGE SETUP INSTRUCTIONS:

| | |
|---|---|
| **# of Pages:** | 1 |
| **Dimensions:** | 11 x 8.5 inches |
| **Margins:** | .5 inches on all sides |
| **Orientation:** | Landscape |
| **Other:** | Draw a rectangle that measures 9 inches wide by 5.5 inches tall. Place the rectangle in the center of the page. Place the contents of the billboard advertisement within this rectangle. |

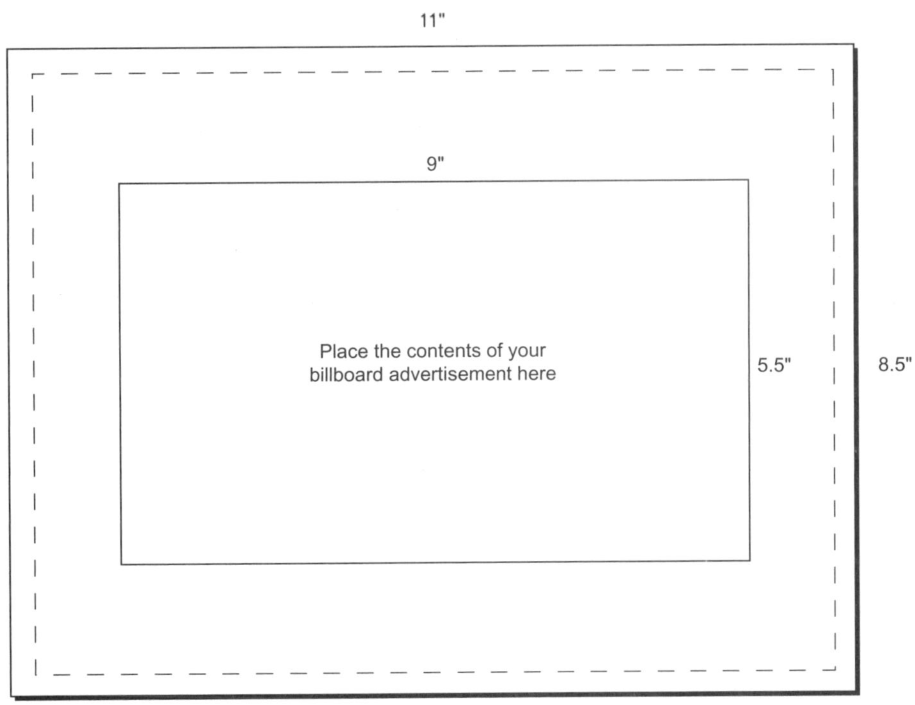

# About Stonehenge's Billboard Advertisement:

The members of Stonehenge knew that the billboard advertisement would be their ticket to generating new fans. The band members went with a simple, yet effective design for their billboard ad. Below is the final design of Stonehenge's billboard advertisement.

*The final design of Stonehenge's billboard advertisement.*

# PART 6: THE ENCORE

## (EXTRA CREDIT)

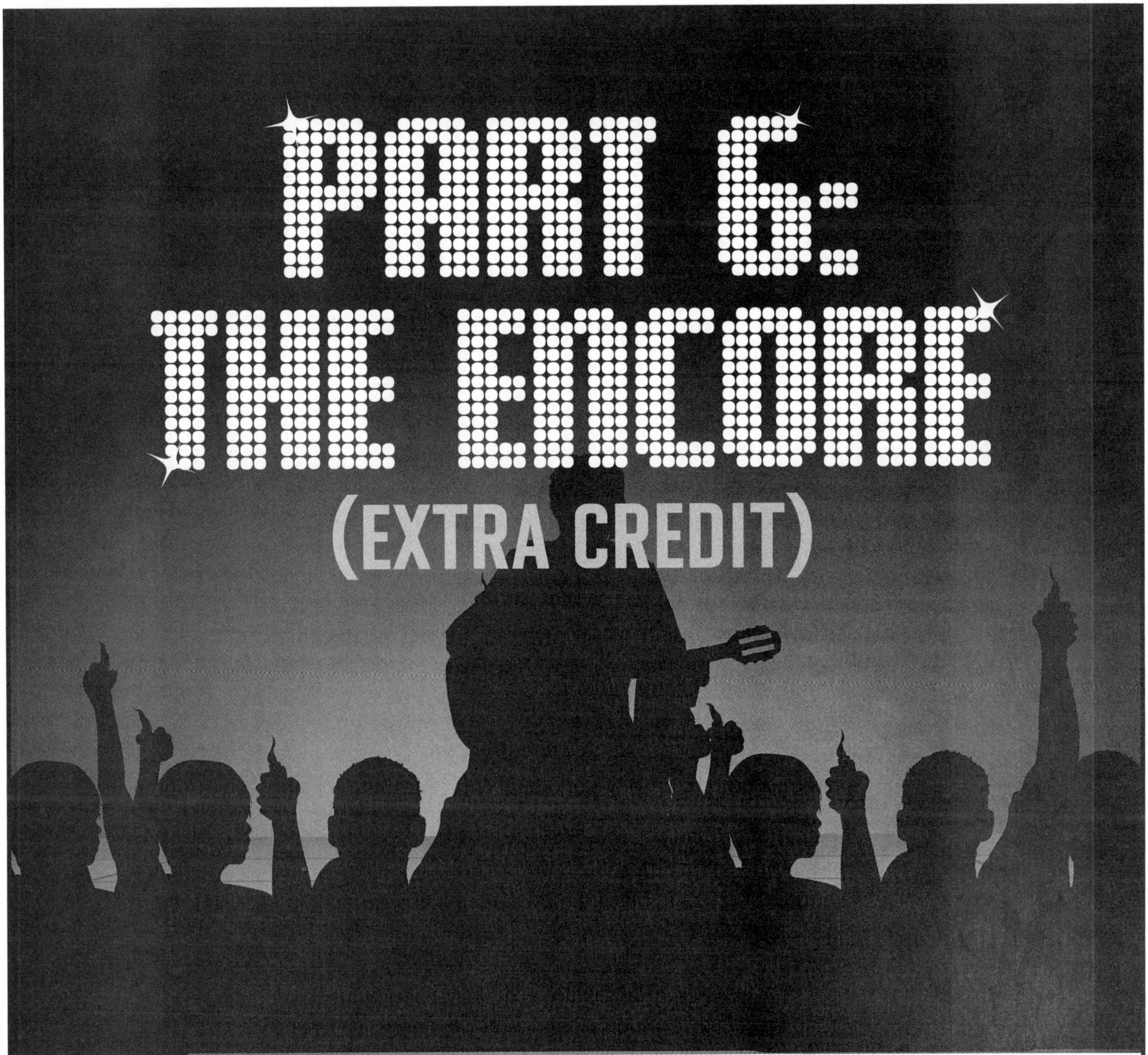

CONCERT TOUR
DESKTOP PUBLISHER

### PROJECTS INCLUDED:

Project 17: Design a Backstage Pass
Project 18: Create a Tour Bus Design

# PROJECT 17: DESIGN A BACKSTAGE PASS

Approximate Completion Time: .5 - 1 hour

## OBJECTIVE:

To design a backstage pass for your concerts

## PROJECT OVERVIEW:

The best part about being in the band is to be able to give people passes to see you backstage after your concerts. Family members, friends, or groupies all want to get backstage and check things out. Use your desktop publishing software to make a great looking backstage pass to distribute to the select few who will get to meet your band backstage.

## GETTING TO KNOW WHAT YOU'RE DESIGNING:

A backstage pass is a special ticket that allows the holder access to backstage areas before, during, and after the concert. Backstage passes are usually larger than normal tickets and worn around the neck so they are easy to spot.

## STRATEGIES AND DESIGN TIPS:

- Since the backstage pass has a limited amount of space available, all important information should be in proportion with all elements.
- Use a maximum of one or two fonts (typefaces) on your backstage pass.
- Use a font (typeface) that is easy to read.
- The overall look and design of your backstage pass should match the image of your band.
- The band's logo should be the most prevalent element on your backstage pass.
- Review the backstage pass designed by Stonehenge in the "Spotlight on Stonehenge" section to get inspiration and ideas for designing your own. *Remember*: Use your own creativity and design skills. Do not copy Stonehenge's backstage pass design.
- Use the "Concert Tour Document Planning Form" to plan the layout and design of your backstage pass on paper first.

# Part 6, Project 17: Design a Backstage Pass

## INSTRUCTIONS:

1. Using your desktop publishing software, create a new document.
2. Save the document as "Backstage Pass" to the "Concert Tour DTP" folder.
3. Follow the Backstage Pass Page Setup Instructions provided on the next page.
4. Include the following on your backstage pass:

> **REMEMBER TO PLAN YOUR DESIGN ON THE DOCUMENT PLANNING FORM FIRST!**

- ☑ Your band's name and/or logo
- ☑ The text "Backstage Pass" or a similar headline
- ☑ The text "Present this pass to a security staff member after the concert. You will be escorted backstage to meet <your band name>.
- ☑ Additional text and/or graphic images that will help enhance the design and appearance of the backstage pass

5. Format the size and placement of the text and other elements on the backstage pass so that they are in proportion with each other and project a professional image.
6. Carefully proofread your work for accuracy, format, spelling, and grammar.
7. Resave the document.
8. Print a copy of the document.
9. Write your name and "Project 17 Backstage Pass" on the document.

# BACKSTAGE PASS PAGE SETUP INSTRUCTIONS:

| | |
|---|---|
| **# of Pages:** | 1 |
| **Dimensions:** | 8.5 x 11 inches |
| **Margins:** | .5 inches on all sides |
| **Orientation:** | Portrait |
| **Other:** | Draw a rectangle that measures 2.75 inches wide by 4.75 inches tall. Place the rectangle in the center of the page. Place the contents of the backstage pass within this rectangle. |

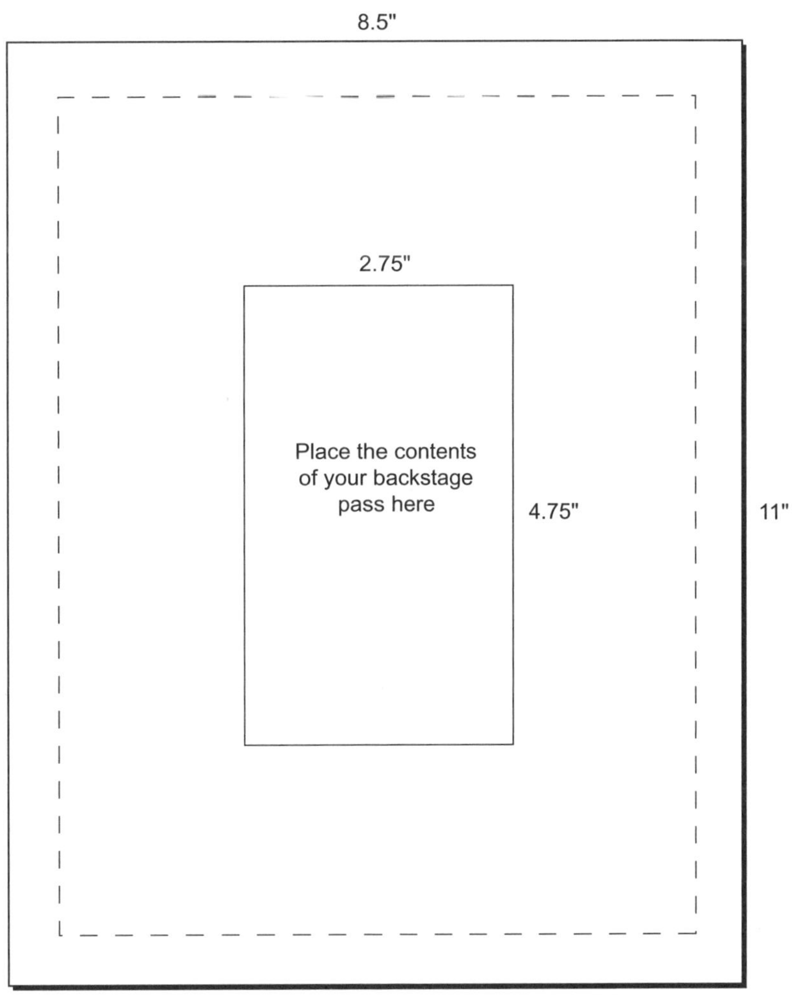

## About Stonehenge's Backstage Pass:

Stonehenge wanted their guests to feel special and privileged about going backstage to meet the band. The final design of Stonehenge's backstage pass, shown below, certainly accomplishes this task.

*The final design of Stonehenge's backstage pass.*

# PROJECT 18: CREATE A TOUR BUS DESIGN

Approximate Completion Time: .5 - 1 hour

## OBJECTIVE:

To create a design for one side of your band's tour bus

## PROJECT OVERVIEW:

Now that your band has made it big, you're going to want to travel in style in your own customized tour bus. In this project, you get to let everyone know who you are while traveling. Use your desktop publishing skills to create a cool design for the side of your tour bus.

## GETTING TO KNOW WHAT YOU'RE DESIGNING:

Tour buses are used to carry band members, stage crew, and equipment around while traveling from city-to-city during concert tours. The bus is usually decorated with the band name, logo, colors, tour name, or other information.

## STRATEGIES AND DESIGN TIPS:

- Focus on creating a tour bus design that can be seen easily from a distance.
- Since most people will see your tour bus while it's moving, your design should be easy to read and fun to look at.
- The band's logo should be the most prevalent element on your tour bus design.
- Use only one or two fonts (typeface) in your design.
- The overall look and design of your tour bus design should match the image of your band.
- Review the tour bus design created by Stonehenge in the "Spotlight on Stonehenge" section to get inspiration and ideas for designing your own. *Remember*: Use your own creativity and design skills. Do not copy Stonehenge's tour bus design.
- Use the "Concert Tour Document Planning Form" to plan the layout and design of your tour bus on paper first.

## INSTRUCTIONS:

1. Using your desktop publishing software, create a new document.
2. Save the document as "Tour Bus" to the "Concert Tour DTP" folder.
3. Follow the Tour Bus Page Setup Instructions provided on the next page.
4. Include the following on your tour bus design:

REMEMBER TO PLAN YOUR DESIGN ON THE DOCUMENT PLANNING FORM FIRST!

- ☑ Your band's name and/or logo
- ☑ Additional text and/or graphic images that will help enhance the design and appearance of the tour bus design

5. Format the size and placement of the text and other elements on the tour bus design so that they are in proportion with each other and project a professional image.
6. Carefully proofread your work for accuracy, format, spelling, and grammar.
7. Resave the document.
8. Print a copy of the document.
9. Write your name and "Project 18 Tour Bus" on the document.

# TOUR BUS PAGE SETUP INSTRUCTIONS:

| | |
|---|---|
| **# of Pages:** | 1 |
| **Dimensions:** | 11 x 8.5 inches |
| **Margins:** | .4 inches on all sides |
| **Orientation:** | Landscape |
| **Other:** | *Follow the steps provided below* |

**Step 1:** Using the rectangle tool in your desktop publishing software, draw a rectangle that measures 7 inches wide by 3 inches tall (this rectangle represents the side of the tour bus).

**Step 2:** Draw a second rectangle that measures 2 inches wide by 2 inches tall (this rectangle represents the front side of the tour bus). Position the smaller rectangle in front of the larger one as shown in the illustration below.

**Step 3:** Using the circle tool, draw a perfect circle measuring .75 inches in diameter. Fill this circle with white (paper) color (this circle represents one of the wheels of the tour bus).

**Step 4:** Select the circle and copy and paste it so that you have three circles on the page. Position the three circles (wheels) in the approximate positions as shown in the illustration below. Bring the circles to the front of the rectangles.

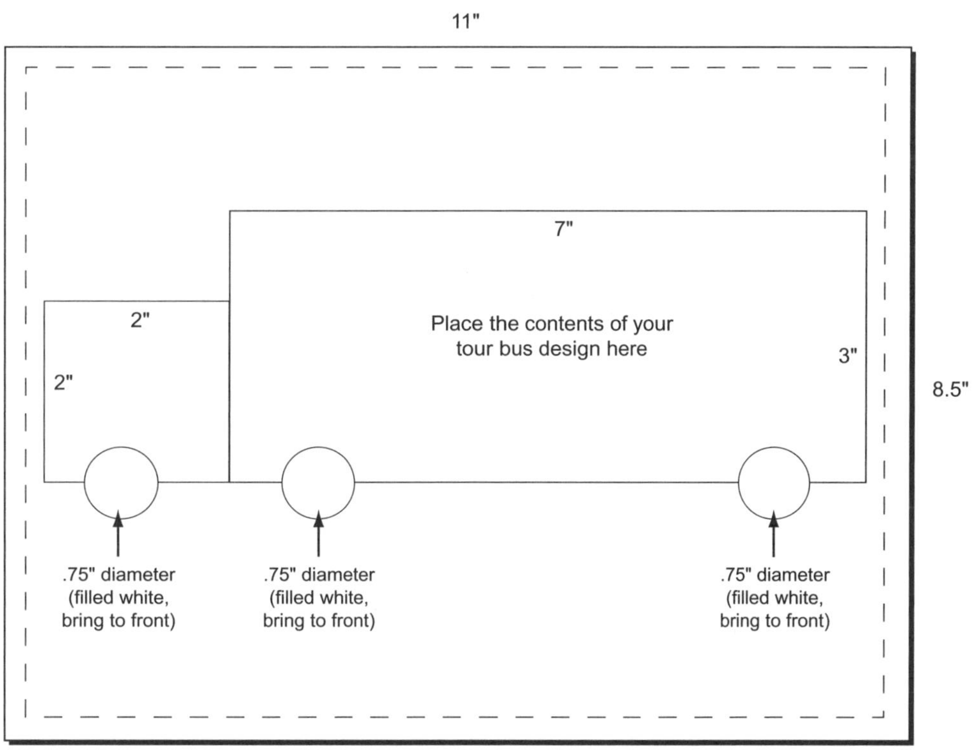

## About Stonehenge's Tour Bus Design:

With the new tour bus design, fans will know that Stonehenge is coming to town. Here is the final design for the band's tour bus.

*The final design of Stonehenge's tour bus.*